In My Own Skin

Kirsten Schowalter

The subtlety of life is rich. It's so rich. Each little bone, the articulation of occipital condyles, the toes and the capacity for balance and movement, stability and mobility. It's rich. It's a source of study, fascination, meaning in existence that can occupy a life forever. Each tiny moment produces sensory information that can generate infinite amounts of possibility. What am I going to make possible? What am I going to let exist? What will I create with the possibility that I embody? How often do I distort the possibility that I experience? Can I experience anything without distorting it?

DEDICATION

To Emma Anderson, my friend

To Dave Schowalter, M.D., Ph.D. a geneticist at Mayo Clinic, graduate of St. Olaf College, University of Washington Fellow, Eagle Scout and father.

ACKNOWLEDGMENTS

This book is the first segment of an ongoing project. It documents my life and memories from a specific point in time. Swaths of time passed before and after in a blur, yet one moment is seared in memory with ripples all around me. Writing unpacks it, decompresses it, scrutinizes it from every angle, attempting to find an explanation that doesn't exist.

My family and friends have their own versions of the stories, and my stories have been adapted to honor their interpretations of the past. Their identities have been masked to emphasize this is my imperfect telling of the deep past. This story is a glimpse into the complexity of my reality.

The work I've done to create these pages could not have happened without the support of many communities. To Gretchen for her photography, Aaron for photo editing, Jim for sharing poetic words about the story, and numerous others for reading drafts again and again, to my family for walking with me along the journey, to my friends for motivating me to the charge, and to the duende for seeing the epic battle all the way through: Thank you.

Finally, I'm human, and this book is a testament to a very human experience. In the process, I have tried to remove typos and grammatical errors, but even with diligent editors and spell check, some errors can slip through the cracks. As the next reader, I challenge you to join in the creative act of storytelling and reach out to me if you find an instance of misplaced punctuation or letters in the book. I look forward to co-creating with you.

Welcome

Walking through a forest of redwoods, I noticed the trees grew in clumps. One stump or dead tree was surrounded by a growth of new trees in a circle around it. Family circles is what they are called. It's like a show of solidarity, support, and community around both the end of life and potential new growth. Together, as one, in honest existence around the family circle.

My family has a pretty tight circle; my mom describes my three sisters and I as her four pillars. She says there's an energy about us that's greater than each of our parts. People can feel the sparks when we're together.

Our family circle is just like the redwood trees. We don't have lightness in us because that's all we are. We have lightness in us because we know the darkness, the end of life, intimately, and we choose to let new growth exist as we are. The greatest lightness is complete appreciation of exactly what is.

We learned over time our family circle, the energy coursing between the synapses of our fingertips, isn't for our benefit alone. No. We make the circle bigger. We scooch over and make a space for you too. There's always room for more in the circle.

I used to think there was only one fact from the hiking trail that didn't translate as a metaphor into my life. This was that that a trail exists for the hiker to walk along. Life doesn't have a known path for you, I thought. Poet Antonio Machado writes "*se hace camino al andar* [you make the path as you walk]."

The magic of the circle though, of the scooch over, is that there is a path in life. There isn't a determined path for me to walk on, but sitting in the circle together, here right now with you, I see there's a path because people have traversed this way before. The path is the footprint of their journey, those before and after. Welcome to the journey. It's here for us to share.

So, grab a spot, a comfortable seat around the circle. Who wants to share a story first? You? Me? We?

There, right then. That's where we'll start. A time ago. In a memory. Let's unpack that moment, bruises and all, and from there only time in the circle will tell.

Black

I woke up that morning to the sight of wooden beams above my head and the sound of something dragging along a cement floor. The beams were dirty and at each intersection there was a spider web or two, some beautiful, some peculiar, but mostly not what I wanted to see while lying in bed. When I was young, I had a nightmare that recurred over and over again. I would see a version of myself sleeping peacefully in my pineapple posted bed and slowly the pillow underneath my head began to move. Over the top of the pillow would crawl a giant tarantula that prowled pedantically until it covered my face and smothered me until I no longer breathed in peaceful slumber.

Needless to say, the spider webs I woke up to that morning were not encouragement to stay in bed.

I heard the sound of something dragging again, and realized my back was sore and tight from the hard, top bunk I had been sleeping on. I looked over the edge of the bed and saw my parents beginning to pack our bags and load them into the car outside the cabin. Getting up meant *work*.

One glance back at the spider webs, however, and I leaped down from the top bunk like a flailing gazelle.

"Good morning, Kirsty girl. How did you sleep?"

"Leave me alone, Dad."

3

I began shuffling through my dirty clothes to find something partially clean I could wear, which turned out to be a brown ribbed tank top and knee-length jean shorts. I packed everything I had brought with me to this Northwoods Minnesota cabin for the week and threw it in the back of the car.

"Kirsten, stop that. We need to pack the car carefully so everything will fit."

"It's not my fault we have too much stuff."

Lucky for me I would be sitting in a crowded car for the next who-knows-how-many hours. At least we would be in the direction away from this place. I returned to the cabin to see my little sisters slowly roused.

"Kirsten, help Heidi get dressed and pack her bag."

"Seriously, Mom? She is seven. She can find a shirt and pants and put them on herself." I didn't want to be anywhere near this place.

"Kirsten, stop that. Help your sister."

After everyone was dressed and the car packed, I grumpily jumped into my seat.

Harrumph. Let's get this over with, I thought.

Mom asked Dad, "Dave, why don't you drive the car around and we will stop in the main hall for a quick breakfast before we hit the road?"

What?! We were staying around this place long enough to have breakfast and see all the people that we'd spent the last seven days with? We were going to do the long, drawn out goodbye with people I really didn't care to see again after my parents had gotten me out of bed to get driving before it was too late into the morning. I check the clock: 7:45am. Really?

"Kirsten, you can ride with me over to breakfast."

Good, I thought, because I am not moving from this seat. Of course, our drive was at the speed of snail, alongside my mom and sisters for a bit, and then passing them and running into the other campers heading for breakfast.

The entire week, Dad had given me relief from the camp with him. He needed to check his email about a paper he had submitted for publishing, so was going to make a run into the coffee shop 15 miles away. Did I want to join him for some company? He was going to get some live bait for fishing at the local One Stop 10 miles away, did I want to come with him and grab an ice cream while we were at it? I shouldn't have been angry with him. In fact, I had been grateful all week for the excursions away from the camp that he gave me, but that morning I most certainly was angry, and I didn't appreciate any of his relief tactics. We finally pulled around to the main building parking lot and I turned to get out of the car. Dad wasn't going to let me get out of this one.

"Kirsten, what's going on with you this morning? We just spent a great week here on family vacation."

"Just leave me alone, Dad. I don't want to be here. I don't want to see anyone here."

"Kiiirsten."

With that we walked into the main lounge. Even though it was barely 8:00 in the morning, the place was bustling with people. The buffet line was steaming with hot pancakes and alongside sat trays of morning pastries. Dad and I ambled down the sloped floor to the beginning of the line. My mom and sisters had already gone through and grabbed a table. Mom sat trying to convince Heidi to eat instead of playing with her food, while Allison and Lily were stuffing lukewarm, rubbery eggs down their throats in order to go run off to their friends for the last few moments before we left. I reached the front of the line and just grabbed a lemon poppy seed muffin. Dad did the same.

By the time we made it to the table, Heidi could not sit still any longer and ran off to a far corner of the room. Another family we knew walked into the building. My sisters waved at their three kids, the same ages, ran off with them to play again; breakfast forgotten. The parents joined my parents and I at our table just as some other parents finished going through the breakfast line and came to join the 'adult' table too.

Oh no. Parents. They will talk for *hours*. So much for getting on the road quickly.

I slowly picked at crusty rim of my breakfast muffin. I tried to ignore the parents' conversation and lose track of time.

"Good Morning, Schowalters! How did you sleep?" one mom asked.

"Hasn't it been just the best week?" her husband added.

"Oh yes, that fishing competition was quite a highlight, Dave," she finished. They were wishfully hoping my parents enjoyed the week enough to come back next year.

After longer than I would have liked, I finally began to hear the telltale signs of the adult conversation coming to a close.

"Yes, well. We've had a great time this week. Thank you for inviting us to join you. Now today, we've got a long drive ahead of us," said Mom.

"Karen's right," Dad added, "we better start pulling everyone together to hit the road. We need to stop at her parent's place before dark."

My parents began the slow metamorphosis from the lounged sedentary chair posture to sitting forward on their seats to standing, calling my sisters' names as they did so. The running around the room came to a halt as Allison was asked to wring in the kids and head to the car. The other parents slowly came to a stand as well, and the Minnesotan goodbyes began. The lingering saunter up the ramp, emphasizing for the third time in conversation the fun that was had that week, giving well wishes for safe travel, and reiterating the value of the connections made during the time together. Once at the car, it all began again, this time accompanied by hugs.

"Karen, thanks so much for coming up with the family," the other mom said to my Mom again. "Dave, safe driving, and, girls, we will see you back at school in a few weeks," she finished.

By the time we finally piled into the car, the crowd continued to wave and yell.

"Goodbye!"

"See you back at home in Rochester!"

"Thanks for the great week!"

All right already!

With the clump of people disappearing behind us, Dad hit the gas and we accelerated back into civilization after a week in the woods. We drove past the little town that had been my refuge with Dad from camp, and with each passing mile I felt more relaxed.

"All right, girls. We've got a long drive ahead of us. Why don't you take a little snooze?" said Dad.

That sounded good to me. I could ignore the world around me and just let my anger dissolve in the nothingness of my sleep. I maneuvered to my right side as best I could, swinging my legs into the middle aisle of our Toyota Sienna, and rested my head on my hand balancing on the armrest. 9:26 am. And then the only life I knew went black.

It's personal

In life, the big memories are turning points, dividing our experience into segments. Before September 11, 2001 and after; before the earthquake of March 11, 2011 and after. For me, the large events of the 90s and 2000s which divide collective history are important, but not so profoundly influential in who I am and what I do. I remember the day, I remember the fear, I remember the confusion, but even though I remember, it wasn't personal at all.

On September 11, 2001, I was in third grade with Mrs. Schneider. In order to practice our multiplication tables, we had to recite flashcards to the teacher. Each day there were two chances to recite the flashcards to her, and after enough multiplication recitations we won stickers, eventually leading to treats. The first time we could recite was in the morning before school. The second time was during any break of the school day, and after the second time, we had to wait until the next day for more sticker-winning opportunities. That day, the one the United States cannot forget, I barely had time for my morning multiplication recitation before class began. We were talking about something boring, when I saw my mom's face at the door of the classroom. Mrs. Schneider called me from my seat to go speak with Mom.

"Kirsten, go pack your backpack. You are coming home with me."

"Why Mom?"

"I'm going to get your sister Allison from the 1st grade room. Hurry up and get your things together."

Without further argument, I collected my red and yellow paper folders, one for spelling words and one for math homework, and put them in my backpack. I grabbed my uneaten cold lunch from my cubby, and walked out of the room. My mom had already retrieved Allison and was running back toward me as I did.

"All right, girls, quickly. To the car."

"Mom, why are we leaving school?" I asked again.

"Is it a snow day?" Allison chimed in hopefully.

"We will talk about it when we get home."

Walking into our house moments later, the television screen was still turned on from when Mom ran out of the house to pick up Allison and me. I saw a building on fire, the plane, the smoke over and over again. I didn't understand what happened. Why was something on the TV so important and dangerous that I had lost my second chance at reciting multiplication tables?

A big moment like this, as much as I can remember the urgent tug on my arm when Mom pulled me out of school or the confusion I felt for why I had to leave so rapidly, it did not touch my life personally and I did not feel an impact that changed the way I lived every single day. Maybe this is because the events happened in places that only existed in my imagination. They didn't exist outside of the TV screen and the words people said.

I think everyone has events of her own that have shaped the course of individual history. Before College and after; before Marriage and after. For me, the segments of my life are most deeply divided by: Before Erin and after. Before the Accident and after.

Even before 9/11, I had been to funerals and seen death.

Before I was born, my parents lost a child, and I was reminded that I wasn't necessarily the oldest. What would it have been like to have a big sister?

I had also lost great-grandmothers. My only association with them was as the elderly women in the nursing home whose lap my parents made me sit on. When they died, I saw the women lying in their caskets, and my Farm Grandma kneeling beside my great grandmother's coffin, picking up what could have been doll hands for how stiff they were, to pray a rosary after the memorial service. I didn't feel the tears at my eyes like everyone else did.

It was only a matter of time before that changed.

Down at the end of the street where we lived in Marshfield, WI were the best friends to everyone's family: The Allmans. Rob and Judy, the dad and mom, knew the ins and outs of town, quickly becoming an indispensable resource for my parents. They had three daughters: Grace, two years older than me, Amanda, one year older than me, and Erin, my age exactly. Even though Amanda and Grace were older than my sisters and I, they became fast friends with my younger sisters. Erin and I became best friends. We took ballet class together. And jazz. And lyrical. We joined the same Brownie troop and made homemade ice cream together for our summer badges, kicking a bucket of ice around the school playground encouraging the cream to harden. We jumped on the trampoline in the Allman's backyard most summer evenings. Whenever we could, we were together.

During the school years, Erin and I attended different elementary schools. Regardless of whether we saw each other that day or that week, the next time we were together Erin and I could laugh and laugh until our cheeks were red as tomatoes and gasping to catch our breath. One birthday, my parents caught our laughs on film. In the photo of Erin and I next to my cake, we are pink with joy and contentment.

At Christmas of December 2001, my family did our usual routine of driving from one part of MN to spend a few days with my mom's family and then stopping back home for Santa

Claus' visit, before jumping in the car again and driving to Milwaukee to see my dad's family. It was just a few days after the holiday when we finally got home to stay. It was late, and the house cold from the furnace being turned down. My sisters were asleep in the car as we pulled into the driveway. I woke up to bring my things inside, and felt the cold tile beneath my feet. I went in search of slippers in the room the four of us shared, quietly though because Dad was laying Heidi in bed. I went downstairs to find Mom on the phone. After she hung up, Dad descended and we both looked at the blank face Mom wore.

"Mrs. Engell called from across the street. She left a message saying to call her back."

"Did you?" my dad asked.

"I just got off the phone with her. She wanted to tell us the news in person."

"What?" he prodded.

"The Allmans were in a car accident."

"Where? When?" he continued.

"Before Christmas. They were driving to visit their family in Minnesota on a road along the edge of a steep cliff. The road was small and a semi-truck was driving at them in the opposite direction. There was barely room for both vehicles to begin with. The semi hit an ice patch and knocked their car over the edge. They didn't fall far."

"Are they ok? Where are they now?"

"Rob and Judy are ok. Minor injuries. Amanda too."

"Erin?" I finally chirped in. My stomach dropping even before I knew the answer.

"Erin died on impact. She was sleeping in the back with her head against the window right where the semi hit the vehicle."

My world stopped.

"Grace was hurt badly too," my mom continued. "They took her immediately to a hospital, but she never woke up. She died a day later."

Emptiness.

My only other memory from that night is sitting upstairs in my parents' bed with the light on, and them comforting me, each other, and Allison as we all tried to let the news sink in.

"I wanted to tell you the news in person," Mrs. Engell had said. Is there any way to render such news?

From that moment on, I have felt that death has always had a way of coming back to touch me periodically. Personal or impersonal, there's frequent reminders. It's perhaps the curse of life that death keeps coming around, but I'd say it's actually a gift. If we didn't die, we wouldn't live. Reminders of death are, yes always, reminders of sadness, personal or impersonal, but they are not that alone. Reminders of death are reminders of the preciousness of life. We can't take life for granted, because it isn't always going to be there. In the book *One Straw Revolution,* author Masanobu Fukuoka writes: "If you want to get rid of the idea of death, then you should rid yourself of the notion that life is on [the other] side. Life and death are one."

One

I knew from the moment I felt it this was not something I had ever expected for my life. One minute I was sleeping, anger, frustration, and teenage angst dissolving into mist, and the next there was this pressure. It was like we'd sped up. But on the other hand, it was also like hitting a brick wall, going 60 mph and coming to a complete stop in the blink of an eye. Maybe it felt that way because that's what it was.

In May, Mom and Dad had spent hours at the Toyota dealership deciding on a new family car to purchase. Our Ford Expedition was done for, and our '88 Toyota Camry was sputtering more often than we liked. It's not surprising then that Dad decided to negotiate a bit of a deal, and purchase TWO cars at the same time, when Mom had only walked in the store with the intention of buying one. Within a few days, they'd test driven, considered, negotiated, and purchased a light blue Toyota Sienna and forest green Highlander hybrid. The next weekend, we had our local dance studio's Spring Recitals, and several people commented as Dad or Mom pulled up to the auditorium roundabout in the shiny new cars.

Just a few months prior to the new car purchase, Mom registered the entire family to attend Family Camp at a popular YMCA camp a few hours from our home. We could sail, ride horses, hike, eat s'mores by the fire, sing songs, learn about bugs, and, my Dad's personal favorite, go fishing. There was even a competition during the week to see who caught the biggest fish.

At camp, there were two ways the evenings went: either, we retired when the sun set from exhaustion; or, we stayed out next to the brilliant campfire, watching the flames dance and sharing stories more profound than ever expected. One night, we chose to retire early. Sure, we'd stayed around the fire for a while, but after several long, activity-filled days, my parents preferred to pull cranky children away for a night of longer sleep rather than continue to fight against the impending exhaustion. Our family had a cabin to ourselves, each girl getting her own bunk bed, and my parents moved two beds next to each other for a larger, parent-sized bed. After brushing our teeth and visiting the outhouse with a flashlight, swatting mosquitoes at our knees and ankles as we walked, Mom and Dad tucked us in bed. My parents settled in their parents' bunk, and Mom read aloud *Harry Potter and the Deathly Hallows*. The rhythm of her voice eventually brought us all to sleep, calmly and quietly in the night.

Crash!

The next thing we knew there was a loud crash and jostling very nearby.

"Lily? Are you ok?"

"Where is the canoe paddle?!" she responded urgently.

"Canoe paddle?"

"Where is the canoe paddle?!" she continued.

Softly a chuckle let out into the room followed by a whispered, "Karen, can you believe it? She fell from the top bunk, stood up, and is still sleep talking!" The chuckling continued.

"Come here, Lily. Let's get you back up to bed."

"Where is the canoe paddle?!"

"I'll tell you what? We can go for a canoe ride in the morning, but right now is time for you to keep sleeping. Righty, spritey?"

With minimal grumbling and resistance, Dad encouraged Lily to return to her post on the top bunk. To Lily's embarrassment, word of the midnight canoe paddler made it around the camp within 24 hours.

With the week of camp behind us, on Saturday, August 11, 2007, we set out to drive home for the last two weeks of summer before school.

Then, our new Toyota Sienna hit the brick wall.

The dark pressure left one moment of calm in its wake before the chaos of the collision occurred. We had been driving on a two-lane highway within half an hour of camp, and just as Dad followed the curve of the road to the right, another vehicle was curving from the opposite direction.

Wham.

Just like that.

Head-on collision.

They told us afterward that the truck actually drove on top of our car as it hit, tipping over and landing in the ditch. We were spun counterclockwise and ended facing forward in our lane once again. Aside from the truck in the ditch, we looked as though we were exactly where we needed to be. There was barely evidence of a skid.

When the force stopped, everything went limp.

The force had glued me into position, and as soon as it was gone, I began to slide, fall. I opened my eyes to a blurred composition of images both strange and familiar. Our car was still our car, but glass was *everywhere*. I could see the shape of Dad's body in front of me in the driver's seat. From deep inside me, I wheezed and moaned at the same time, a sound I'd never heard before. I tried to take a breath, but couldn't. I lay there for a moment, without air and detached from any physical sensation except something tight around my neck and stomach. The thought passed in my head, "We are just like the Allmans now."

The sudden memory of friends and my life as it had been

stimulated my survival reflex. I needed *air*. I couldn't breathe. I was pinned against the seat by something, and I wasn't going to breathe if I didn't make it stop. For the first time since the force, I was roused out of my stupor, jerked upward and was pinned down once again around my neck and stomach. "The seat belt," some unconscious part of me realized, and my hands found the red release button before my head had even fully realized the cause of my suffocation. With the release, my entire body sprang up.

Free from my seat's grip, which saved my life in one moment but almost drained it from me in the following, I heard the sound of my mom's voice yelling from outside the car.

"Girls! Get out of the car! Now! Run away! Run!"

I didn't know why we had to run, but her cry gave me a direction and a sense of urgency to move.

'Maybe she wants to make sure we are out of the car in case something is going to hit us again. Maybe there is a fire,' I thought.

As I stumbled from my seat, I ran through glass on the floor from the windshield, and unattachedly noticed a stream of blood flowing down my leg.

'What happened?' I wondered. 'I don't feel anything.'

Glancing back toward my seat, I saw Dad still sitting in the driver's seat. His back was straight up, his body stunned, but the way his head limped over the air bag aimed toward his chest gave me a suspicion that I couldn't place. It was strange he hadn't affirmed Mom's command to run, but maybe he knew something I didn't.

As soon as I moved, I realized I had left Lily and Heidi in the back seat. Allison ran from the car almost immediately after Mom, and the way Mom pleaded we run caused me to act and fast. I was out of the car, tumbling toward the green of the grass before I had time to make sure my little sisters had made it out of the car too. It hadn't even crossed my mind that they might need help. Somehow, they had managed to follow me out of the car, tumbling alongside me on the roadside where the gravel pebbles digging into my head, ankles, knees, and side felt comfortable.

Solid ground.

First, we moaned, and then someone started to cry. I tried to comfort whoever it was, wisps of "it's ok", "you'll be ok" sliding out my mouth without hesitation. Lily's cries became long, painful, wails, and I couldn't find any strength inside me to pick myself up and help her. My body was anchored to the ground. She was in *pain* and I didn't know how to do anything about it.

A raindrop landed on my hand, and I heard more begin to fall, prickling against my pebble pillow.

Carbon, nitrogen, and oxygen

One of the first and last times that I got to spend with my dad, just him and I, in which he treated me like a grown up with ideas of depth and maturity, we discussed beavers. Dad knew beavers from the cabin at Pelican Lake.

We made homemade sandwiches for lunch, after picking out our favorite bread, condiments, and chips. He sat down at one end of the table, the end that Mom normally frequented, and I sat at the exact opposite spot, his normal position.

"Kirsten, I have an idea," he said squarely. His tone said this idea was not a spur of the moment thought of brilliance, but rather one that had been on his mind a lot.

"What? What is it?"

"There's a lot of talk about ethanol and new sources of fuel for cars. You remember from when we were buying our cars in May, right?"

"Yeah, I remember. The corn oil."

"Although I admire the effort to investigate new fuel options, I think it is problematic that we are growing corn, taking what was once used for food and making fuel from it, and then leaving all the rest of the plant in the field to decompose. Like plant garbage."

"What would you do with the plant garbage?"

"At the most basic level, Life is carbon, nitrogen, and oxygen. I think there has to be a way to take that plant garbage break it down into the most basic chemical compounds and then figure out how to take those basic molecules and make more fuel out of it."

"How would you do that?"

"Well, the places making this fuel must have to break down the corn somehow, and I suppose you could do the same thing with the plant garbage until it gets to the same compounds as the corn, and then mix them together. That way, we could use the whole plant in the fuel rather than just kernels."

"All right, I buy your idea. Let's do it. Let's figure it out and make it happen, Dad. Where do we begin?"

He raised an eyebrow at me and winked.

"Beavers. I think we need to know more about beavers."

"Why?"

"Just think about it, Kirsty girl," distracted from his lunch now, he pulls forward in his chair. I can tell he is really excited about this idea.

"Beavers use their teeth to cut down trees. How can they do that? There must be something in their saliva that helps in breaking down the bark or stalk material of the plants they chomp on. What if we could find that enzyme, and we used that to break down the leftover corn stalks? Could it work? Could we find a natural way to break down that plant garbage into something the ethanol people can use?"

"Whoa."

"Life is just carbon, nitrogen, and oxygen, after all."

Stable

The last time I had closed my eyes, the clock read 9:26am. By 10:15am, other cars arrived at the scene, phoning ambulances and emergency help. Lily, Heidi, and I lay in the ditch, while Mom and Allison were somewhere else. I couldn't tell you where. I couldn't tell you how long it was before the sound of sirens reached us and an unfamiliar paramedic came over to me and asked, "Who is in the most pain?"

"Take my sisters. Please help them." I said. Lifting my head, and feeling the pebbles from the gravel come with me. Before I could think again, Heidi and Lily were whisked from my side onto stretchers and into the ambulances and helicopters parked nearby. Laying my head back down, I was alone.

"Kirsten, are you ok?" I heard someone pass by to check on me. All I could do was moan in response. Another undefined moment of time passed, and the sounds of people and sirens diminished. It became calm.

Eventually, another paramedic returned with a stretcher for me. He or she, I can't remember, rolled me onto the stretcher and carried me into what appeared to be the last ambulance. I saw my mom come running towards me.

"Kirsten, I'll see you at the hospital, ok?"

"Ok." I responded in the nick of time before I was loaded

into the car and the doors shut behind me. With the little vision I had, I was pretty sure there was not anyone familiar in the ambulance with me.

The paramedics began asking me lots of questions, basic questions.

"What's your name?"

"Kirsten Schowalter."

"How old are you?"

"14."

"How many sisters do you have?"

"3."

"What day is today?"

"Saturday."

On and on, so many questions. With each answer, what little breath I had inside escaped bit by bit. I needed more air. Within seconds of thinking it, an oxygen mask floated down from above as if of its own accord responding to my mental beckoning and covered my nose and mouth. For a moment, my body went rigid, presuming the mask would prevent air from reaching me, but quickly I felt a stream of air flow toward me, and I relaxed.

With a constant supply of air to reach my lungs, I began to only desire to shut my eyes and return to the sleep that I had been so abruptly disturbed from. Maybe going to sleep would undo the strange series of events from when I read 9:26am on the clock. Maybe I just was really tired. Either way, it was the worst of nightmares because the paramedics wouldn't let me sleep.

"Kirsten, you need to stay awake."

Why?

"Kirsten, keep your eyes open."

Why?

"Kirsten, can you answer some more questions for me?"

No. A thought floated across my mind that perhaps they couldn't let me sleep because if I did, I would die. They would lose me. I formulated a message, thinking I needed to reassure them: I'm not going to die if I close my eyes. I promise. But before the words left my mouth, another part of me was shocked at the abrasiveness of the sentence.

Since when was I so close to death? How was I so calm thinking about dying? I hadn't connected it at the time, but I think it had something to do with having been so recently at a thin place; one of those moments in time where the boundary between here and whatever is out there opens for just a moment, something passed from one side to the other. I was not afraid.

Before I could continue arguing with them, we arrived at the hospital. As they wheeled me into the emergency room, it was clear there had not been a lot of action there during the morning so far. The quiet, although refreshing, was disconcerting.

'Where is my family?' I wondered, but didn't have time to dwell on it because a whirlwind of motion occurred around me immediately. I was taken into a white, sterilized room, and lifted from the gurney to the table. Everyone left the room, and a single doctor returned. He or she asked me if it would be ok to take off my clothes and put me in a hospital dress. I didn't care. I don't know if I answered. My body still felt too heavy to move, and as long as I didn't have to do it myself, it didn't matter to me.

Expecting to hear the sound of my pant's buckle and zipper, I was shocked when scissors sliced at the bottom of my capri pant leg. I had put on these jeans and plain brown tank top because they were the only clothes I could bear to wear after a week of dirty camp clothes.

I guess I won't be wearing these again, I thought, as the scissors continued up my body, and for the second time this morning my body sprang upward in release.

Another whirlwind of motion began and I was examined, both with human eye and machine. After being prodded by several people, I was claustrophobic in the MRI.

"Breathe in and out for me, Kirsten. Listen to my voice. Breathe in, breathe out. Very good." I listened to the voice of the technician coming through a microphone.

They returned me to the same small, sterile, white room and for the first time since I arrived, I was alone.

The moment wasn't long enough to begin to formulate a thought. I heard a movement at the door, and saw the face of my aunt Lisa as she walked in the room. I was so happy to see her, a face I knew, I felt my eyes filling with tears. There was light inside me, and I blurted out, "Where is my family?" Joy whizzing from my mouth to know they were near.

She responded, "Your mom is with your sisters at another hospital. They were taken to an emergency room too."

"And where is my dad?" I asked eagerly.

She looked back at me silently. Her face didn't change; it was the same composed, cool look that she had entered the room with.

"He's dead." I said.

She held the pause for a moment, not denying or affirming my words.

"I'm not supposed to say anything to you about it until you are in a stable condition." She said. I didn't care.

"I knew it," was all I could say back to her.

Lightning proof blinds

When storms come in the Midwest, there's a pattern. First, it gets hot. Too hot, too fast. It's nice for a moment and then everyone complains about the heat. Complaints are always the first indicator of change. After the heat, comes the rain. It rains, it stops, it drizzles, it rains. Then the colors start to change. That's when I know a storm is coming.

A good thunderstorm is the combination of all the elements. The water over the earth, and the wind driving the pressures that build up the fire, that electricity in the clouds. In science class, we learned that weather was the result of pressure. Warm fronts and cold fronts interacting with each other. The closer together the warm and cold fronts the more pressure between them. The wind would blow faster, and thunderstorms happened.

Now, whenever I experience a thunderstorm, I have that map of a giant red H for high pressure slowly moving across the green land mass with spiraling lines coming out from it as it reaches the blue L for low pressure with its own set of swirls. As a kid, I remember these times looking outside the window and the world was green, amazing yellow, or rose, fascinated by this experience of the elements. For some reason that power up in the air makes me feel close to the things I cannot control.

It's like the poem that used to hang in my parents' bathroom.

It was the only place upstairs that had no windows. Walking in I passed my parents pajamas hanging behind the door and smelled my dad's Old Spice aftershave hanging from them. It felt like a comfortable place, warm within the bowels of our house.

When we lived in Seattle, my mom would wake up early to take a shower, and as soon as I detected the water spritzing from the spout, I would sneak down and wait for her inside the bathroom wrapped in bath towels. There is something about bathrooms that gives me comfort. Maybe it's the loneliness; we can wash ourselves clean. We can let anything that clings onto us slide off into the drain far away from us and take in the energy of the newness that comes into us.

In that upstairs bathroom hung an image. Two people walked along a beach, looking over the footprints behind them, the path of the one's life. At the times when his life was most difficult, there was only one set of footprints.

The one asked the other, "Why did you leave me when times were most trying?"

And the other, it turns out God, responds, "When you see one set of footprints, that is when I carried you."

That's the *something beyond* that I like to acknowledge in thunderstorms. It is the something that carries me when I can't walk myself. It is the something that will guide me, when I am not sure what anything means.

When I was little and a thunderstorm came, I was afraid. The way the wind made our house rock felt like we were in a tree house; the tall one that was going to get struck by lightning. Worst of all, I was going to watch it happen.

My room didn't have any curtains. As soon as there was lightning, I awoke. I heard the rumble that stirred through the frame of the house and I could not sleep.

I pleaded with my parents for curtains. I couldn't see the thunderstorms because they made me scared.

As it were, my request was not high priority.

After more thunderstorms than I would have liked, Dad purchased blinds to install on my window. However, installing them was also not a priority, and so it wasn't until the next storm came when he heard me scared again, that he went to fetch them. Just as the storm was in a moment of calm, he stood next to the window and screwed the blinds in above my window.

"There we go," he said when finished. "Lightning-proof blinds.

"You know, Kirsten, the storms really aren't scary. So, I have made the blinds special so that if you ever want to watch the lightning you can just turn this rod, and they will open up. They will still protect you, but then you can see past them and watch the storm."

It seems silly now that a pair of blinds could feel like protection from the most uncontrollable world beyond, but from that night on, I was intrigued. I could wake up and watch the storm, and that pair of blinds made me feel safe. Those spaces, the bathroom and in my room behind the blinds, they were my safe spaces. They were the places that let me go into myself, reconnect me with the elements, wash me clean of the shame, embarrassment, and humiliation I experienced, and they were the places that return me back to me.

I was in a storm, and where were my lightning proof blinds?

Stitches

A while later, the doctors returned to my room and explained my situation to Lisa. She left with them, and another person came into the room. He or she sat down at the end of the bed, and began speaking with me. As this person did so, he or she cleaned my foot, wiping my ankle with alcohol. They took a tweezers and began picking the glass out of the gash I had barely noticed, threading a needle, and sewing my skin. I don't remember feeling anything except the tug. Once, twice, three times at the same spot again and again. It didn't hurt though.

"All right, you've got 6 stitches in your foot. Five across the top and one that's inside the gash, ok?"

"Ok."

As soon as they left, Lisa came back into the room, this time accompanied by my uncle Jack. He spoke with me for a moment, and then began making jokes, trying to help lighten the air around me.

"You seem to be the only person in here today. Guess you get all the attention, don't ya?"

It wasn't long before the emergency room personnel returned and took me from the room I was in and back into the ambulance.

"Kirsten, we are transferring you to another hospital for the night."

I looked for Lisa and Jack.

"They are taking you to the same place your mom and sisters are."

"Ok." I said.

A car ride and several more rides through hospital hallways landed me in a large room with four hospital beds, one with each of my sisters and I in it. My mom stood between us. I'd never been in a room like that before. It felt like it was made special for us, because nothing ever came in packages of four. Just us. We made the rest of the world, socks, underwear, gum, a multiple of 4, even when it was 21 strips of gum and 4 girls to divide between.

A few hours later, we were transported from this large, family sized hospital room to smaller rooms several floors above. I lay in a white bed, with stiff and coarse sheets wrapping me in tightly. The window to my right gave view of the sky, just beginning to clear after a rainstorm.

Seeing the sky for the first time since I laid on the side of the road was nauseating. The world did still exist. I wasn't in some strange dream scene of chaos, long hallways, physicians in white coats, and scratchy sheets. The sun had moved in the sky and time was passing.

"Kirsten?"

I turned away from the window to see my mom enter the room.

"Hi Mom."

"Kirsten, are you hungry? We are going to sleep at the hospital tonight. The doctors want to keep an eye on you to make sure you are ok to go home, same with your sisters, and so they are going to bring up some food."

"I don't want any food."

"Kirsten, I know you aren't hungry, I'm not either, but you need to eat something. Mashed potatoes, maybe? Would that taste good?"

With her suggestion, she reminded me of the out-of-the-box mashed potatoes Farm Grandma made when we visited. They were pasty and salty, but something about the idea of those mashed potatoes sounded delicious.

"Do you think they'll have the potatoes like Farm Grandma makes?"

"Probably."

"I'll have some mashed potatoes then. And, do you think they have ice cream? The little cup ice creams with the sprinkles that we get from the Schwanns man?"

"I'll ask."

"Ok."

Mom left the room just as quietly as she had entered. She looked tired. I still don't know what my mom confronted that day. I felt as though the only thing I wanted to do was sleep, and I had spent most of that day in a bed.

"Hey! Look who it is! How are you, kiddo?"

I was alerted from my reverie by a familiar voice. Our church youth leader walked in the room.

"Joshua? What are you doing here?" Pastor Linda followed him into the room. I felt confused seeing familiar faces when I had no idea where it was.

"We came as soon as we heard. We just got out of the car."

"Oh."

"Are you ok?"

"Well, Joshua. You know, I am going to need to get my license very soon. I know I am only 14 and that you need to be 15 to get a driver's permit, but I will have to get one the moment I turn 15, because Mom is the only driver in our house now, and I will have to help with getting groceries and running errands and taking my sisters to school and picking them up from school and making dinner…"

"Kirsten. What are you talking about?"

"…my driver's license. It's important that I get one soon and fast because I have to help my mom take care of my sisters and now we only have one driver in the house. I don't know how we will manage, and we will just have to make do for a little while, but eventually I think I could practice enough so that…"

"Kirsten. Stop."

I hadn't spoken that fast or as much all day.

"Kirsten, you are light years ahead of what's going on right now. Are you ok? How are you feeling?"

I paused for a moment to realize how quickly my mind spun out of control. Seeing Joshua was the first time I verbalized concerns for how this one day would shape my future.

Finally, I responded. "My neck hurts a lot, and this paper and tape they have on it is really itchy."

"What happened there?" Joshua asked.

"The seatbelt," I began.

"Oh," he sighed.

"It burned me here." I finished.

"I am so sorry, Kirsten. And, I didn't mean to diminish your concerns about driving. I just can't imagine how you can think about that right now. If you ever need help with rides, we will figure it out, ok?"

"Ok."

"We are going to go say hello to your sisters, all right?"

Just then, I heard a knock on the door. A nurse poked her head around and asked if she could bring in the tray of food.

"Yes." I said to her, and turning to Joshua again, "Ok. I will be here."

"Ok, see you in a second," he said as he walked out the door.

"Hi Kirsten. You asked for mashed potatoes and ice cream?"

"Yes."

As she set them on my bed, I learned the tray clipped into the bed to allow eating without any difficulty. The warm potatoes smelled appealing. Ice cream made me smile.

"Is there anything else I can get you?"

"No, thank you."

"Would you like me to turn on the TV?"

"Sure." I hadn't even realized there was one in front of me.

"What would you like to watch?"

"Um…" I mumbled as she turned the TV on and began to flip through channels. "That, yes, sure." I eventually responded.

"Ok, remember, you can press the call button on the side of your bed if you need anything else, sound good?"

"Yeah."

She exited the room leaving me alone with my potatoes and ice cream. I looked down at them again, and as I picked up a white plastic spoon to dig in, I realized, 'This is the whitest meal I have ever eaten. Uh. I don't know if I like it.'

As much as the food tasted good, the first bite of potatoes verifying, yes indeed, the hospital made potatoes from the box, I couldn't stare at the white, blankness of the tray in front of me. From food, to packaging, to utensils, to napkin, everything was white and blank. It made me sad.

I looked back up to the TV. I had chosen a news channel, and as I did, the broadcaster played footage of a car crash. My entire body tensed as I saw the clip, and I immediately reached for the remote to turn it off. I couldn't watch it. I couldn't see that. It had happened to me. How was that possible?

The Inevitable

I was twelve. We lived in Rochester. I had my own bedroom that looked over the front yard and the cul-du-sac which was our refuge. Even though my room could have been considered exposed to the world, it was blocked by an overgrown birch tree. The tree was so large it threatened to break through the walls of the basement with its roots. It had already caused cracks in the driveway and nearby sidewalk, and grew more every day. This tree blocked my window. I could see some things, and I presume people from outside could see in if they looked hard enough, but it was a thick mass of green, brown, flaky leaves that turned my room into a place of solitude.

For the previous owners of the house, my room had been an office. There were two closets, a series of bookshelf cupboards underneath the window, and a desk that had been installed into the frame of the room. This meant the few furniture items I had, bed, dresser, bookshelf, needed to fit like a puzzle in the remaining space of the room. My twin size pineapple bed fit either perpendicular or diagonal from the wall on the left side. Those were my two options. Although the diagonal was an interesting interior decoration choice, I came to prefer the perpendicular position for its square and yet angled division of the space.

Aligning my bed this way created a narrow space between the bookshelf cupboards under the window and my bed, just wide enough to open the doors of the cupboards and put things inside. It was also just wide enough for a young me to sit in and feel safe while still experiencing the light or dark of the world.

Other times, for example during the years when I wanted to be the best ballerina I possibly could, I would sit in the narrow space with my legs spread apart in a wide second position and try to push myself to sit closer and closer to the wall. I thought, if I keep stretching and sit here long enough, eventually I will become more flexible. Once I started those stretches, I couldn't stop there. I came up with new ones every time I thought my legs or hips were going to fall apart. I was a practicing contortionist with the help of that little nook.

The night before I turned 13, June 24, 2006, I sat in this space with the lights out, looking out the window. I sat for only a moment before I started crying. I cried and cried, I tried to cry softly, but I couldn't stop the tears.

I had spent years listening to my parents talk to me about teenagers who had too many hormones running through their bodies to think clearly, or make productive decisions about their lives, succumbing to peer pressure, and falling away from their parents, becoming pregnant and not being able to make a living for the rest of their life as they try and raise a child that instead of being a joy was in fact a signal of weakness, failure, and stupidity. Teenagers got piercings, tattoos, drank, did drugs, and were generally unpleasant people to be around, or so preached my parents while they presumed I still valued their opinions and ideas. And they were correct. I heard them. Every single word.

I sat in my nook crying because I knew the moment I turned thirteen, I would no longer be a child. I would be a teenager. I would not be a master of my own devices and the next time I would come out of the slug that was the teenage experiences was when I turned 20, too old for me to comprehend. I didn't want to hate my parents. I didn't want to disappoint them. I was afraid of being pulled astray into the dark abyss that was a teen. I was afraid no one would notice or come for me to pull me back to who I was and the family I belonged to. I didn't want to grow up; leave the darkness of that night, and move into the light of morning. Everything would be revealed. I would be a teenager and there was nothing I could do about it.

An it

The next day, Mom wanted to try to get us home. She said it would be better for us as a family to be back in our own space. The sterile hospital environment made it challenging to feel anything other than disorientation. The doctors cleared me for departure, and I was loaded into my aunt Carol and Terry's large red Yukon for the long drive home. What other car could we use? We didn't have ours anymore.

At first, we each sat in the rear passenger seats. The movement of the car was a bit unnerving, all of us too recently remembering the roaring halt of our drive the day before. Within minutes, Lily began to complain of back and stomach pain. It started quietly, she whimpered and Mom tried to calm her. I sat next to her and smoothed her hair, rubbing her tummy to help it feel better. Rapidly, her whimpers turned to cries to screams of agonizing pain. We immediately pulled over and fashioned the third seat into a bed where she could lay down. It didn't help though. Her screams became more piercing, and we didn't know how to help her, to stop the pain. Lily has always been the accident-prone child. From age one and potential meningitis, to broken arms, pulled out toenails, and stitches to close the gash on her forehead, she has a high tolerance for pain. She doesn't complain until something is really painful. Her screams in the car were indication that something was very wrong.

In the minutes of trying to help Lily remain calm, and the rest of us as well, we suddenly had arrived at the St. Cloud hospital. Mom ran into the Emergency Room to alert them of our arrival. Sounds of a chopper in the air above commenced moments later. Lily was whisked from her backseat bed, onto a gurney, and into the helicopter. Mom ran alongside Lily, who now scared of her destination, cried harder.

A few minutes later, Mom ran back out to the car to inform us of the decisions inside the ER.

"They are going to fly her down to the St. Mary's Hospital Emergency Room. I want her home. I want us all home, so they are going to fly her there so she is as close as can be."

"Are you going with her?" aunt Carol asked.

"They won't let me. I promised her I would come find her as soon as I could."

"Ok, well, you can ride home with Jack and Matt. They will take you as quickly as possible to Rochester. We will come along behind with Kirsten, Allison, and Heidi."

"I want to get home to see Lily too." Allison chimed in. "We have to go fast."

"All right," uncle Terry responded. "I'll do my best for you, Allison."

Returning to our respective means of transportation, Allison, Heidi, and I sat close together, arm in arm, the whole ride, wanting nothing more than the security of each other. I couldn't sleep in the car. There was no way I could close my eyes and trust my world would not turn even darker and venture in scarier directions. The drive seemed to last an eternity. The transience of the 60 mph speed limit feeling like the same speed of limbo we had last existed in before our lives changed beyond ever comprehensible. 24 hours ago, Dad had driven us out of the camp driveway. Now, he was dead. Where was his body? Who had it? Will I get to see him or it again? Was it an it now? Is that what death does to us?

Dear Kirsten, Please help your sisters and your mom. Please don't be scared because God is watching over you.

Kirsten- love is forever. Wishing you comfort. Your friend always.

Dear Kirsten, don't forget I love you.

Kirsten- We are thinking of you and want you to know how much we care now and always!

Dear Kirsten, I'm so sorry for your loss! You're in my thoughts and prayers. Though I haven't lost a father, I'm sure it must be very hard. I'm thinking about you.

Giving and Receiving

When we are little and don't want something, we can cover our ears, and close our eyes, curl into a fetal position. It's a simple way to physically separate ourselves from the external forces and come back into a safe, warm, familiar place. If I close my eyes, whatever is out there doesn't exist, right? If I plug my ears I won't hear that bad noise, right? If I don't let you help me, then I don't need help, right?

Help is a two-sided coin. In order for one person to help, another has to be helped. There's a giver and a recipient. My natural posture is to help. I went on mission trips in grade school to help with disaster relief, or I babysat my cousins to help my aunt and uncle move. I help people.

After our accident, I wanted to be alone. But the people started coming.

During our drive home, some friends of my mom called her to ask what they could do for us in Rochester.

"Our house is a mess. I'm so embarrassed to think of all the people seeing it like that. I think our neighbor has a key if you want to try and get in." She answered.

At the ready, Mary and Barb went to find the key, vacuum and dust our house. Our main floor boasted two living rooms, one primarily filled with furniture from City Grandma. In it, there was a rather aerodynamically tipsy, antique lamp which stood on a side table. Mary, in a moment of unfamiliarity with the space, made a quick turn to her left and knocked down the rose-colored lamp, effectively shattering it to pieces.

"Oh no." She looked at Barb with horror. "For all I know this was Dave's favorite lamp. And I just broke it."

Within a year, Mary gifted my mom a new lamp, almost identical to the one she broke. When my mom received it, she said, "What is this?"

"It's the replacement lamp. The one I broke."

"Oh for Pete's sake," Mom responded, "that lamp has been an accident waiting to happen for years. Don't worry."

In the months and years later, we still received offers from people to do or give us something. "We don't need that. We don't want that. Why do people keep giving us these things?" I told my mom, frustrated beyond belief.

"Kirsten, they are hurting too. They want to do something and it makes them feel better to do something for us. It's ok that you don't want it, but accepting their help is us helping them."

Putting it that way, she effectively peeled my stubby hands away from covering my three-year-old eyes, plugging my little ears, and helped me stand up, opening my heart to receive what people gave.

At first, I could do this easily because I knew I was a grieving person.

Then, after I should have "gotten over my dad," it started to feel like accepting help also was also accepting a preconceived notion of who receives help. The widows, the orphans, the homeless, the hungry.

Even though Mom is a widow, or I am a child without my dad, receiving help sometimes feels as if I am asked to put on clothes I have outgrown. Not because I have "gotten over it," but because as I grow the hurt holds a smaller proportion of who I am.

I am still grieving, and that won't stop. But, instead of "getting over it," I keep practicing. Even though I don't want to impose. I don't want to take favors, an important part of being someone who wants to help people means that I also need to accept help that others give to me. Poet Jim Bodeen says, "When you find the cookies, they're always for you."

Fault

My dad worked at a computer business when he was growing up. Between my grandpa and him, I can always remember their excitement about a new computer, software, or gadget. For Dad, this fascination also expanded to making slideshows. He made them for anniversaries and weddings, special occasions, or fun. He would put pictures together, using them to make a statement in conjunction with his music choices. He was an artist like any other I would define, someone who used their medium to present a view of something that might otherwise not have been seen. We girls then also decided we wanted to make slideshows too. Increasingly, as school projects offered the options for videos or we found an occasion, we learned how to do them too.

It makes sense that the moment Allison got back to our house after a grueling drive home, she started a slideshow. It was her, Dad's, and our way to process what had happened and to understand what was going on.

While I laid on Dad's side of my parents' bed just laying, she spent hours at the computer, putting together pictures from the week we spent at camp alongside the monumental moments in our lives. She was going through a Miley Cyrus phase at the time and chose "I Miss You" to use in the slideshow.

After the ruckus of the day had quieted and Mom, Heidi, and

I were alone at the house, while Lily was at the hospital, Allison gathered us at the family computer, which sat at the desk in the kitchen and living room space. This was the space where we were a family. This was the space where we convened as a new, different family for the first time to recognize the end of one era. We were heading somewhere very uncharted into the future. This moment marked the end of our family of six.

As the first note of "I miss you" began to play and the first picture of Dad lounging at a picnic table at camp, we cried more and harder than we had in the last hours. He was so close, and yet so far. We had just heard his voice, just seen his face the day before. The chaos of the accident had paused for a moment and the reality of our new life first dawned on us.

I felt comforted by our space, but I knew something was missing. I was confused: whole and empty at the same time. With the revolving door of visitors bringing lasagna, homemade mac and cheese, and hot turkey sandwiches, it was hard to tell exactly how much the emptiness would hurt us until everyone left. I spent many of my days upstairs away from the crowd. I had been reading *Jane Eyre* before we left for camp, and I was determined to finish it. I didn't enjoy the book, but forced myself to read as a way to do something. Pass the time. Every once in a while, I descended from my hiding place.

"Kirsten, come sit with me on the front porch," called my aunt Lisa. She came with us after my stay in the hospital. She was an Army helicopter pilot and was more accustomed to that edge between life and the abyss of everything beyond control than I was. She was one of the few family members I felt I could let into my hurt, because she had been with me in my lowest moment.

"You all right?"

"Yeah, I was just trying to read. This book is so boring, but I want to finish it."

"Kirsten, it's ok to know that you are in shock right now. I've seen before in my colleagues in the force before. The world seems to run in slow motion, sound is foggy, and your vision detached. I just want you to know I'm here for you. Whatever you need. You tell me, ok?"

"Ok. Thanks, Lisa."

"Oh, and one more thing."

My eyes looked back with question.

"Uh, this is kind of embarrassing, but the doctors, up at the hospital, you know. Well, they asked me to watch you for, uh, a report."

"What are you talking about?"

"Um, Kirsten, I need to know the first time you, uh, go number 2. They want to make sure everything is working right inside, and that's the best way. So make sure you are eating, and just give me a little signal when it happens, ok?"

"Oh. I see. Ok."

"All right. That's all I was supposed to do."

"Lisa?"

"Yes?"

"Do they know what happened on Saturday? Like how our car accident happened?"

"Well, they have special investigators on the case, Kirsten. It's confusing because there were barely any skid marks or signs on the road to indicate what happened between the two cars. From their current reports, they think your car crossed the line and spun around to end up facing back in the proper place in the lane."

"How can they say that?!" I exclaimed. "Dad didn't cross the line! He didn't do anything wrong!"

"Kirsten, calm done. It's all speculation at this point. Whatever they decide, however, is what will be officially recorded. Your dad crossing the line doesn't mean he is, I mean was, a bad person."

"But they say it's his fault?! It's his fault he's dead? He's dead! He would never have hurt anyone. He would never want to leave us like this. It's not his fault. He didn't do it."

"Kirsten. Your dad loved you. He was a good, responsible person, and even if they report the accident as his fault, it doesn't mean he wanted to die or hurt anyone. I don't know if they told you this, but his body was destroyed on the inside. There was so much damage, the coroner couldn't tell whether he had a heart attack or stroke or some other medical complication that might have caused a split second of less attention on driving. We don't know."

"It isn't his fault. He didn't do it. He's dead."

"I will certainly keep talking with you about this, Kirsten, as I learn more about the police report. Even though, we may not like what the report says, I am not arguing with you about your Dad. He loved you, and never forget that."

To show your love in my own way

Help me Jesus everyday
To show your love in my own way
In all my work and all my play
In what I do and what I say. Amen.

My mom tells a story of when my dad decided he wanted to have a special bedtime prayer for his daughters each night. Dad sat down criss-cross-applesauce in front of the bookshelf in our bedroom. He wasn't often sitting this way though, so his legs didn't quite cross all the way under him, leaving him more in a sitting criss-cross open legged position. He pulled a book down off the shelf, and began to rifle through the pages. I, the ever eager reader, immediately joined him on the floor, pulling one book off the shelf, looking at it, disposing it on the floor and returning to the shelf for another one. I created a pile of strewn books *No, David!* on one side of the room and *Goodnight Moon* on the other, while Dad kept reading through his one book.

"Kiiiiiirsten. Look at the mess you are making. We have to take care of the books, not throw them around," Dad teased me. Smiling back at him, I stopped mid action of pulling out the next book, sat down in my own criss-cross applesauce, and picked up the book that happened to be lying next to me to begin looking through. I watched Dad as he continued his skimming, and pretended I was equally as engrossed in my book as he was in his. One, two, three pages later I was antsy again; this time throwing the book back onto my pile and climbing over to sit in Dad's applesauce lap.

"What do you think about this one, Kirsty Girl? *Now I lay me down to sleep…*" He began.

"What are you doing?" I interrupted.

"Reading, Kirsten, listen."

"*The Lord I pray my soul to keep…*"

"Reading what?" I persisted. This book wasn't *No, David!* Or any of the other books Dad would read and I recite the words along.

"Prayers. We are looking for a bedtime prayer." He said. "What do you think of this one? *From this place…*"

He read prayer after prayer to me. "That's nice, Daddy." "Sure, Daddy." "What's that mean, Daddy?" I interjected.

"Here we go, here we go, Kirsty."

"What?"

"*Help me Jesus every day to show your love in my own way. In all my work, in all my play, in what I do, and what I say. Amen.*"

"But what does it meeeeeeean?" I groaned, squirming from my seat in his lap.

"Kirsten, it's a reminder to live like Jesus did. He forgave us, he was kind to people, he didn't hit his baby sisters or poke her in the eyes,"

I gave him a looked filled with sass, are you trying to tell me something, Daddio?

"What is going on in here?" Mom exclaimed as she walked into the room with the aforementioned younger sister.

"Allison boo!" I squealed jumping up from Dad's lap on the floor and reaching for her as Mom set the baby on the floor. As soon as Allison was in reach, I began petting her head and face.

"Kirsten, stop that." Dad chided. "What did we just talk about? Come here, let's read our prayer to Mom. Come 'ere."

"Okaaay." I groaned. Moping back to Dad's lap, I laid sideways over his knee, while Dad began the prayer again. "*Help me Jesus everyday...*" "Help me...Jesus...love today..." I followed his lead. More or less.

From that moment on, *Help me Jesus* was our bedtime prayer. When we were downstairs at the end of watching a movie, or goofing around on the staircase after our parents had told us to go to bed three times already, we knew they were serious when they started walking towards us reciting "Help me Jesus everyday..." Bedtime was coming whether we liked it or not. Later, after we finally learned the words, sometimes Dad would tease us. We'd wait patiently in our beds for goodnight kisses, and as he walked in the room he began to recite the prayer.

"*Come Lord Jesus...*" He'd start the wrong prayer.

"Daaaad."

"What? What's wrong?" He acted surprised and offended.

"*Help me Jesus every day...*" we began again, and he smirked back at us, knowing we'd caught him red handed. Every once in a while, when the prayer became truly routine, we'd sit down at dinner and begin "*Help me Jesus everyday...*" finishing "*In what I do and what I say. Amen,*" only to realize minutes into the meal we'd recited the wrong prayer, no joke intended!

What was it? A routine. A simple routine. In cases like this, is also was a reminder of how washed away from the present we could be, absorbed entirely in our own thoughts we hardly recognized the words coming out of our mouths. Dad took the time to choose the prayer, trying my patience as he did so, because it was also a mantra. A simple mantra to live by.

We create routines and rituals for a reason. On the one hand, they are a way to place a sense of order and prioritize practices that embody the values we believe are important. For my dad, this was about teaching his daughters a way of life that was caring. On the other hand, it's helpful to have a rhythm when it's time to adjust to the inevitable: change.

Regardless of our car accident, this bedtime prayer routine was going to change as we aged. We humans all understand the same mourning for times past and the nostalgia of what was.

When Dad didn't recite, "Help me Jesus" to me anymore, I focused on pronouncing the words fully myself. What was I really saying? What does it mean to show love in what I do, say, work, and play? How was Dad living the message of the prayer in the way he parented me? My sisters? How he was a doctor? Spoke with his patients?

Change provides a rich and sometimes painful process of increasing awareness of why we believe what we believe, why one routine practiced these beliefs in a particular way, and how it was effective (or not) in the past context. Despite of the fierce and howling winds of uncertainty during change, it's the rhythm of routine that gives us a place to hold on to and find some sense of continuity in being.

Routines

In those days, I moved through the world without head or heart. I went places, talked to people, and answered many questions, but I have no crisp, clear memories of what happened. I don't remember sequence, how many days passed, or why we did what we did. Routine and ritual were all we had.

One day, after we had been home maybe two or three nights, Mom took us down a road in Rochester where we'd rarely driven. This street, more accurately, this exit off highway 52, I had taken maybe 3 times over the course of the 5 years we had been living in Rochester. As the car turned to the exit, I didn't recognize the buildings we passed, or where we were going. As the fast food chains along the highway disappeared behind us, the road continued through open field.

Eventually, we took a right into the parking lot of a building standing alone. It was regal for the setting. On the outside, it read Ranfranz and Vine Funeral home. The only other times I had been to a funeral home in my life they were filled with fragile lamps, antique furniture, and the smell of moth balls. Elderly relatives mourned the death of an even older relative, and I managed to play with rosary beads in one of the pews long enough to entertain myself until I could remove the itchy tights I had adorned for the occasion in the car as we drove away.

This time, it was hot outside. The sun seared me within seconds, and I walked as quickly as possible to the glass double doors of the building. Walking in, we were greeted by a tall, large, middle-aged man who was the director of the home. A home and yet a place I had never been before. He took us into the main hall for wakes, and explained how the process normally worked. He showed us the room where refreshments would be held, and I was surprised how welcoming the place felt, soft yellow walls, comfortable couches, a few sensible and not overly ornate lamps.

Then, he pulled his keys out of his pocket, and took us into a room on the right that was unopen to the public who would attend Dad's wake. It was sterile. The walls were completely white, the carpet solid grey, and nothing, nothing in the room except for a few folding chairs where we went to sit. I didn't listen as he asked my mom questions about the songs we wanted to sing or who would speak at the wake, how she wanted the casket arranged, and what kinds of flowers to place around the room. I had been in a fog before, but now I was entirely detached from the present moment in a white, endless, stupor, much like the white sheets, napkin, potatoes, and ice cream I'd eaten in the hospital only a few days before. The white was as if everything had been drained out of my surroundings. There was nothing, but blankness, emptiness. A white hole is distinct from a black hole in an important way. With a black hole, at least I know it's sucked in anything that got close enough to its gravitational pull. Entering into the blackness myself, I would find good company with everything else that has been consumed. The white hole, though, is the lack of everything. Everything has been pulled away from the hole, and there is nothing left. Just blank, white, emptiness and loneliness.

Suddenly I heard, "Would you like to see the body?" and I was raised out of my white emptiness. I was suddenly so excited, "Yes, I want to see Dad." Where had he been these last few days? No one had let me see him after I left the car. How did he get here? What did he look like? "Yes, I want to see him."

A door opened to my left, and a stainless steel table was

wheeled into the room. My dad lay with his back flat on the table and a sheet over his body; his head and toes were the only body parts we could see, as if he were a specimen they had already fully examined like the frogs after my 7th grade Life Science lab. We were seeing the finished product of a dissection. *Gasp.*

He didn't even have a pillow to lay his head on.

That's so wrong, Dad doesn't lie like that. He lies on his side, clasping the pillow with both hands, hair mussed up from sleeping and toes crinkled together. As he approached us, or rather the table approached with him on it, because I could see he wasn't moving himself anymore even though it went against all expectations I had of my dad, it hit me: he was white. His skin was pale, translucent, and white. He didn't have the pink, rosy color filling in his cheeks, or the olive skin tones that made him tan not burn in the sun. It was gone. He was white. He was empty. He was white.

At that point, the stupor lifted and although focus returned, I dissolved into incoherence. I cried, stared at this body that was my dad but he was nowhere to be found, and cried, heaved, sobbed. The funeral director watched us patiently, and Mom asked, "Can I touch him?" He responded "Yes."

She walked toward the gray table, and began to rub his feet. I think now, she must have been attempting to bring warmth back into the body of her husband, because she too saw how empty his body was. She rubbed, and meditated over him, as I sobbed harder watching her try to bring Dad back to no avail. His feet didn't warm. They didn't turn rosy. I had to touch him myself to know it was true. I began to move toward the table and grabbed the edge of the sheet. I pulled it back just enough to find his right hand. I reached only one finger first toward his hand and touched his skin.

Cold.

I pulled my hand back, still shocked by the touch sensation that confirmed what my sight had already told me but I didn't want to believe. My finger approached his again, and this time I was shocked by how much the texture of his skin still felt like Dad's. It was Dad's skin. Why was it so cold? In the time it took me to move alongside Dad and touch his hand, Mom had finished rubbing both feet. "Can I move the sheet off his legs?" She asked, "Yes," the funeral director responded. We all watched as she did. *Gasp.*

He was terribly injured. His legs, broken, bruised, and lined with gashes and cuts, were only the beginning. Sobs broke out from my breast again, and the memory of the crash, the pressure, the glass, the *pain* rushed back. And I had been barely injured. I sobbed harder as I thought about how much *pain* Dad must have felt in that moment. He was hurt just like us. I couldn't catch my breath. He legs covered in gashes were only the beginning.

I didn't have the stomach to see any more of this broken body, the one that died, and with it the Dad I loved. The next time I saw the body, the funeral home had covered him in so much makeup he looked as if he were about to go on stage for a theatrical production in which he was actually a black man who had been covered in foundation to turn him fleshy white. It was caked on, and although I couldn't see the white, empty flesh anymore, he looked even more unreal than on the steel table with only a sheet covering his body. In the casket, he wore his clothes, his eyes were closed, and his hands folded as they never were in real life. That moment, a spectator looking at my dad's body as a specimen on a stainless steel table was the closest moment I had with the real him after seeing him hanging over the airbags and listening to his words "Take a little snooze..."

When will we get there?

I loved family road trips growing up. To City Grandma and Grandpa's cabin or to the Farm for Honda rides with Farm Grandpa, my sisters and I would pile into the car with our pillows, coloring books, and stuffed animals, while Dad precisely packed every inch of available space with the bags and belongings Mom had set aside. Mom strapped in our large TV and VHS player around the front two seats.

After one and then another potty check, we would pull out of the driveway with everyone and seemingly everything we would ever need in life. Dad liked driving, and Mom would inform us when we could turn on the TV and when we needed quiet time. Everything felt complete in that moment.

"How much longer until we get there, Daaad?" I groaned. "My legs are stuck and I have to go potty."

"Kirsten, have you taken your nap today?" Dad responded.

"No! I don't want a nap. I'm too big for naps."

"Kirsten, your sisters are sleeping. Don't wake them up."

"Daaaad. When are we going to get there?"

"Close your eyes. Close your eyes, and I will take the short cut, ok?" He said.

"You'll take the short cut?"

"Yes, and we will be there lickety split." He reiterated.

"Ok, fine."

As uneasily persuaded as I was, the deal of a short cut was too appealing to turn down. 'How did he manage the short cut?' I wondered. I imagined Dad taking the car bushwhacking through the fields and forests to get there as soon as possible. What a beautiful thing the innocence and imagination of childhood. I never had any reason to doubt him.

He was hurt;

I dreamt I was with my high school crush. In the dream, he was almost my boyfriend. Almost because we hadn't told anyone yet, but we knew it. It was also a matter of religion. That was a hold up.

I met him at the dark of night in the middle of a snowstorm to go to his church with his other friends and act in a Nativity play. We were the last ones to arrive at the church. It was my almost boyfriend and his friends wearing the suits Mormons adorn for their mission, and an older man already in costume as Obediah, the innkeeper that gave Joseph and Mary a place in his stable. Obediah was the director of the play, and the rest of us had other roles. I was the lead female since there were no other women to play. I did a fabulous job in my role.

Afterward, I began to walk out of the church, proud of my acting when my almost boyfriend's friends came running after me and reminded me each was supposed to be compensated according to the size of her role. In other words, I would be compensated most and I hadn't been paid at all. Obediah controlled the money.

I stormed back into the church and in a moment of feminist indignation I demanded my share from Obediah. The other boys came to my support, and then became vehement, approaching Obediah and trying to grab the money from him, eventually stripping him of his clothes and beating him until they succeeded.

I thought this had become particularly violent and went to ask the now disrobed man if he was ok. I looked down and saw the actor's true face for the first time: He was my dad.

They had beat up my dad.

What's worse they had left him like that and ran off, stealing the money I was to be paid. I was so worried for Dad, but he assured me he would be ok. He said he never gave me pay because he was trying to protect me from the boys stealing it, just as they did. In all my feminist rage, he couldn't deny me, but he knew all along the boys had provoked me in order to take the pay for themselves. They weren't honest and he was trying to take care of me. I trusted the wrong people, and even when I hardly knew Obediah I should have trusted him.

he was gone.

700. That's how many people came to Dad's wake at the funeral home later that week. He was dead and yet it was a wake. It was the largest wake of the year.

From the moment our family arrived, there were people. All over. As I walked into the chapel room of the funeral home where Mom met a receiving line, pews were lined for prayer, and Dad in his casket displayed at the altar, I saw flowers everywhere. Toward the back of the room, someone, maybe my aunts and uncles, had created several poster boards with pictures from my Dad's childhood, growing up, and our family life which had just come to an end. I wandered through the space not really conscious of where I was and how slowly I moved past the decorations. I saw Dad dressed in clothes this time and covered in makeup in what looked like a comfortable bed in the casket. I considered lying down with him. But, the white, the cold from feeling him before persuaded me otherwise.

For a while, I sat in a chair in the front near the casket. I just sat. Sitting, looking at the place, the body, the box, not knowing what else to do. As the line of people got longer and longer, I came to join my mom in receiving the hugs and tears. Some people came for Mom, some came for Dad, some came for me, or Allison, or Lily or Heidi, and it was mildly helpful to separate out lines for a time, but eventually it merged back into one long line of waiting people.

At one point, my favorite middle school teacher came to the front of the line and after speaking briefly with my mom, she pulled me aside and took me to sit up front. She asked me how I was, and what was on my mind.

"My twin brother committed suicide when we were young." She told me. I hadn't known that.

"I'm so confused, and don't understand why this had to happen." I began, and she nodded along, affirming my thoughts had been hers at one time too. As we continued talking, the funeral director came forward to begin a brief rosary ceremony, and our conversation dissolved into the repetitive phrases of "Hail Mary full of Grace, the Lord is with thee..."

As a child trying to understand what happened to her family, I didn't look at the wake and funeral as a process that was helpful for me. It felt stilted, ritualistic, and full of movements that didn't make sense to me.

"I think the ritual is important, because it's in death and the other moments of life when we are in shock and least capable of doing or saying something that we can rely on the ritual process to lead us plodding along dazed through the early days, nights, and weeks of losing a loved one," my mom claims.

I agree with her, and I agree a celebration of life is important. At that time though, the minutes filled with "Blessed are Thou amongst women, and blessed is the fruit of thy womb Jesus..." or sitting trying to read a book in my parents' bedroom felt the same. Neither fit me, it was motion in a blurry lens.

The crowd continued long after the allotted time for the wake, and eventually Mom couldn't take any more receiving. She called an end to the evening, and we must have departed to our house again for dinner that would remain uneaten on my plate. "Holy Mary, Mother of God, Pray for our sinners, now and at the hour of our death. Amen."

My mom remembers the day of my dad's funeral as the worst day of her life. She woke up and knew she was going to bury her husband of 17 years. I don't even remember waking up the day of the funeral.

I must have turned toward my dresser and pulled on the white knit sweater I had set aside for myself. During the previous days, our neighbors had taken me shopping to find appropriate clothes for the wake and funeral. I think they took two of my sisters, Allison, Heidi, and I. I remember purchasing a tan sweater and a pink and brown skirt for the wake, and I could only find a white cable knit sweater from Gap to wear for the funeral. Amy Bentley volunteered a skirt her oldest daughter had, who was five years younger and smaller than I, to wear with it. After we returned home from the mall, she brought the skirt over and insisted I try it on. Unzipping the fragile metal zipper tag that almost zipped right off the zipper, I was able to pull on the skirt, a surprise. Closing the skirt again, though, was going to be challenging, and it turned out if I wore it just below my bottom ribs, it fit. I walked out of my bedroom wearing the skirt and sweater, thinking everyone would notice that 1/3 of the skirt lay hidden under the sweater between my ribs and hips, but to my surprise the crowd of people downstairs, probably comprised of my grandparents, Amy, some other relatives and friends, unanimously agreed the outfit suitable for the funeral.

Early that morning then, I must have pulled on this black and white beaded and flowered skirt. I think we were maybe in a waiting room somewhere at church while people arrived, or maybe we were classically late as my dad would expect of us, because I remember walking into the narthex next to the casket and everyone was already seated inside the sanctuary. My mom walked in front, and I think Allison, Heidi and I must have followed close behind, while grazing our fingers over the edge of the wooden casket rolled alongside us.

Did the brass ensemble play? Did the choir sing? They must have. We filed into pews along with all our extended family, and the service began.

It's hard. It's hard because people do their best to show their support but when there's a hole giving myopic focus to the absence of one person, many hugs barely begin to make it feel full again. It's a weird sort of proportion where the hole from one person eclipses the presence of all the others.

I'm not sure how they came to exist, but during that time someone created large white Styrofoam boards with our names written across the top. All over the white surface, different signatures were written, some with little notes "Lots of love!" or "The Anglins are thinking of you" addressed to Heidi. Scrawled along the bottom of Heidi's in the handwriting of a young child just learning to write the alphabet, is written "I love Dad I love dad."

Seeing the words, I think Heidi must have written them herself. Even though I was preoccupied standing by Mom, shaking hands and receiving hugs, Heidi must have been drawn in to the colored markers on a big white board. I know she was. That is exactly the kind of trouble a young Heidi in a fancy dress would look for. She probably ran through the lobby area of the church with the markers, laughing and screaming as cousins tried to catch her and bring the markers back to the table. "Markers are for writing on paper. Write on the paper, Heidi." What does she write? I love Dad I love Dad. Thinking to herself, "Everyone has been talking about him today. I haven't seen him since we were at camp. I don't know why Dad isn't home. Mom says he isn't coming home. Why? Well, Daddy, I love you." Scribbles of various colors adorn other patches of the white space, for me, looking at the poster brings back the hundreds and thousands of people that showed up for us during those days. So much support. And yet, Dad was missing. Half of our parents were now gone.

Lily was still in the hospital when the funeral happened. Somehow my uncle and aunt figured out how to stream the service so she could watch it from her room. As a way to entertain Lily through her moments of pain, Carol decided it would be fun to call our extended family members seated at the front of the church and watch them nervously reach into their pockets to silence phones, which shouldn't have been ringing in the first place. Lily, almost like a god herself, would look out over the screen of family.

"Uncle Matt. Right there. Call uncle Matt."

As soon as she named her wish, it became command. My aunt dialed the number of the selected family member and they only had to wait moments before the person would jump unexpectedly at the noise coming from their pocket. Lily got to watch it all on camera, laughing hysterically at the chaos she controlled from afar.

Mom didn't know if she wanted to speak or not, but in a moment of silence, she signaled to the head pastor to allow her to step forward and say a few words. She spoke firmly, composed with only a few tears leaking out her eyes, and she made the congregation laugh several times as I know my dad would have enjoyed. At the end of the words, she asked for help in returning our lives to a sense of normalcy, and that with daughters dancing in the Nutcracker, we would need to sell tickets for the performances in December.

We held the record for number of tickets sold that year. And the year after. The next year, and the year after that too. That's how much the community came out to support us.

As she came back to her seat, I felt awe towards her. How was it possible she could say anything at all? Words didn't come to me. I couldn't speak.

After that, I don't remember what happened.

Something Out There

I woke up. My face, my pillow, my blanket wet. Why am I wet?

I'd been crying in my sleep. Again.

My confusion cleared to my dark bedroom. I rolled onto my side, curling my legs to my chest. I didn't have the strength to stop the tears.

Everyone else was asleep. I didn't want to wake them. I didn't go find them. I had to take care of them now. How could I do that if I couldn't even take care of myself?

Then, someone sat down at the end of my bed. I felt a hand press into my back. He rubbed my back, warming me from outside and soothing my tears. The sobs came harder and he kept making circles, constant, smooth, warm.

When the tears were done, I felt the circles on my back stop. The weight on my feet at the bottom of the bed was still there. He was still sitting at the end of my bed. I rubbed at my eyes with my blanket, and looked to my feet.

Someone was there.

I spoke, "Where did my Dad go? Why is he gone?" The tears came again, and so did the hand soothing me. "Why is he gone?"

After the second wave of tears, I wanted to see who had found me in the dark. Who had it been? Whose hand rubbed warmth into my heart? Whose pressure at the end of my bed made me feel I wasn't alone in the dark?

I blinked my eyes clear again and looked to see the person sitting at the end of my bed.

No one was there. I blinked again. No one. But I could still feel the pressure of someone sitting on the end of my bed. No one was there. But he was there. I know he was. Something else is out there for us, because he was there. I would have been terrified if I hadn't felt so sure.

Impaled

I felt like I had been impaled. It was as if part of me had been gouged out; not gently chiseled but forced out of me. When I looked down, I could see through the hole past my liver to the wall behind me. No amount of stitching could close that wound.

I could pretend like I didn't feel it. I could continue my walk and live denying it ever happened. But denial doesn't take away the effects. It's like physics: energy is neither created nor destroyed. Those energies inside me responding to my hurt would not disappear even if I denied they existed. I might have been able to pass them by for a moment, but they came back for me.

More difficult than denial is saying, "Ok, this hurts a lot, but I'm going to try to be myself." Some days it worked. Some days it didn't. It was easy to become overwhelmed with the onslaught of feelings that only a moment ago seemed subdued. It was dangerous, and risky, because it meant I might lose my composure in front of other people. This was the ultimate sign of defeat for me. I did *not* want to show my emotions to other people. I tried to keep up with everyone while being as raw as a patient never closed up at the end of surgery. Every time I was in a crowded space or when I was speaking to someone who wanted to try and help me be ok, inevitably something would hurt. A tender spot seared by unawareness. It wasn't anyone's fault, but it hurt.

I showed up to ballet class in September determined to be ok. I stood next to the barre as if I were going to start some tendus as soon as the music was cued.

False.

I couldn't pointe my foot like everyone else; I couldn't stand on my right leg; I couldn't perform the combinations at the right tempo; I couldn't even do the steps. I was seated watching the class before frappes.

Then there were days when I didn't try to pretend I wasn't hurting. I walked into my high school, moved between classes, and responded curtly to the how are yous, and what's happenings. I lost interest in conversations quickly. Who cared whether our team won the football game on Friday? I don't feel like going to a pep fest anyway. Losing interest in the life that my friends enjoyed turned into losing interest in many of my friends. I became lonely fast. I became bitter too. I had a gaping wound and yet everything was fine as long as I gave smiles and let people run under the assumption they were real. For me, that wasn't fine.

Meanwhile, I kept hurting. It hurt physically. Emotional experiences have physical impacts on our bodies, and physical injuries are emotional ones too. With both, after enough trying it's inevitable that a strong sense of nihilism and fatalism set in when eventually I accepted I was broken.

She Comes Home

Every day during this time, Mom spent many hours at the hospital with Lily. When she wasn't there, another family member or friend volunteered to stay with her so she wasn't alone. Within a few days, the number of people available to continue hospital shifts dwindled.

"I can't believe how unhelpful the doctors are," my mom said walking into the house one day after being at the hospital. "It's like one doctor comes in at talks to us like Lily is a bowel. The next doctor comes in and thinks she's a pile of vertebrae, and yet no one is telling us what is going on. She's also a child. A little girl. A 9-year-old who recently lost her Dad. I wish they would see that."

I didn't know what to say. Lily's condition was still a mystery. One morning she would be much better, and the next she was writhing in pain again.

"Kirsten, would you go to the hospital and visit Lily?" Mom asked me that evening. "I think she is losing hope of healing because she feels so alone. Just think, you, Allison, and Heidi at least have each other here at home. Lily is alone, and no one is helping her feel better."

I didn't want to go to the hospital. I felt like I had barely left the last one where I had entered on a gurney like any other emergency patient. I also couldn't bear the thought of watching my sister in pain. I was so hurt. I didn't think I could handle it. What if she died too?

"Kirsten, will you go?"

"I don't know, Mom. I don't know if I can."

"Kirsten, Lily needs her sisters."

I reluctantly agreed. "Ok. I'll go."

A few hours later, I loaded into someone's car as she drove me to the hospital. Mom was going to stay at home for a little while, and I went to find Lily with a kind friend who volunteered to take me. I remember walking into the hospital. It was clean and bright. Friendly, even. Not what I had been expecting.

The friend, whoever she was, directed me upstairs and down hallways. We arrived at a darkened hallway, with several rooms lining the left hand side. We walked past one with a little boy watching TV, another with a little girl and her family surrounding her, and then we arrived at Lily's room. I could tell because it was full of flowers. Just like our house. It hadn't taken long for the main floor of our house to feel more like a greenhouse than a human abode.

Lily was so small in the bed. She was barely breathing. The friend nudged me in and said she would wait outside while I went to see her. I walked into the room.

"Lily?"

No movement.

"Lily? It's Kirsty."

Still no response.

I walked around from the foot of her bed to along the side. I slid my hand across the sheets until I found her hand. I grabbed hold of it, and for a moment, felt the cool, nothingness of her response. I was about to be worried, when I felt her fingers wrap around my hand too. Suddenly, my fears for visiting her in the hospital were washed away.

What had I been thinking? It was lonely here. Incredibly lonely. How could I have avoided coming to see her? The dark, cool hospital air wafted above us.

"I'm here, Lily. I'm here. It's going to be ok. I love you. You are going to be ok."

Lily and I spent an immeasurable amount of time holding hands. It was like the energy from my body was being transferred to hers, and I could see her remembering feeling loved, cared for, and I wanted nothing more than to give her all I could so she would be ok. I don't know to this day the rollercoaster she rode during her weeks at the hospital, but I knew the day I saw her, she was lower than ever. I ran my fingers through her hair. I rubbed her arms, and just kept telling her I was there.

"I'm here, Lily. I'm not going anywhere."

After that, I demanded regular shifts with Lily at the hospital. I was so excited to see her each time I came in. I could tell Lily would let down her guard, and be real with me about the funny thing a nurse said to her or the annoying test the doctors made her do that morning. She was coming back to life. And yet, we still didn't know what was wrong with her.

One day, she had another x-ray, and the doctors found that her L4 vertebrae was shattered. How could this be? How had she spent weeks screaming in pain between three different hospitals, and no one noticed her back was broken? She was rushed into surgery to fuse several lumbar vertebrae with a metal rod. It was a long procedure, and Mom paced nervously the entire time.

Two weeks later, the physicians concluded that although her back was healing, her continued pain was due to a bowel obstruction. Their conclusion: she needed another surgery. This time they would cut out the obstructed part of her bowel, and sew the remaining pieces together again. Hopefully, it would allow food to move through her system again, and the pain would stop because there wouldn't be build ups stretching her intestines. Once again, we paced during another long surgery, and afterward all we wanted was for Lily to come home.

Was she better yet?

The day Lily came home from the hospital was 6 weeks after

the rest of us arrived home from the car accident. The end of September was upon us, and the leaves on the trees outside the living room window had already begun to turn brilliant reds, oranges, and yellows. I walked in from the high school bus at 3:27pm, and found our living room rearranged.

She sat squarely and stiffly in Dad's brown plaid chair, a cast on her arm and a blue brace that velcroed around her torso to protect her spine. She was smiling, but exhausted. Mom, Allison, Heidi, and several other family members and friends swarmed around her, feeding her ice cream and showering her with other gifts. A process of show and tell began as she unpackaged the gifts she had received in the hospital, the most impressive of which was a diamond ring amidst the many, many stuffed animals. Meanwhile, my mom read the cards from the greenhouse now adorning the main floor of our house. Some were addressed to our whole family; others directly to each of us.

Within half an hour, Lily tired of hearing sympathy again and again. She couldn't stand all the attention, and requested some quiet. With her physical limitations, however, she was not ever going to be left alone. She had to be in very specific positions to maintain the integrity of her back.

When the crowd had cleared, I walked over to her. "Hi Lily."

"Hi Kirsty."

"I'm glad you are home."

"I'm glad to be home too. But Kirsty, it's not home. It doesn't feel like home with all these people, flowers, and something missing. What happened, Kirsty?"

"I know, Lily. It's not like it was. It's not ever going to be the same. This is what you missed in the hospital. It's been very chaotic here."

"The hospital almost seems quiet compared to here." We both laughed at that, remembering how often her IV machine beeped or someone knocked on the door to give her medication, a consultation, or whisk her away for an X-ray.

"Lily, I want to tell you something."

"Yes, Kirsty?"

A few weeks prior, when Lily was still in the hospital with no signs of improvement, we were asked to select Spanish names in my high school Spanish class. The teacher suggested we choose a name that was a translation of our name. As I looked down the list of options, there were none that functioned as the translation of 'Kirsten.' I looked again, and found 'Cristina.' It could've worked, but I had never felt like a Cristina in my life. I wasn't Cristina. I thought about it a little longer, and *de pronto* [suddenly], I knew which name to choose: Liliana. I chose it for Lily. I didn't know whether she was going to live or die. I didn't know how much pain she felt or if she would ever recover and be my quiet, feisty little sister again. When Señor Montes came around to each pair of student desks to write down our chosen names, "*¿Cómo te llamas?* [what's your name?]" he asked.

"*Me llamo Liliana.* [Call me Liliana]" I told him. He gave me an inquisitive look, and wrote the name down on his sheet. "Liliana." He said. "Ok."

As I walked out of class that day, he called me aside, "Why Liliana?" he asked.

"It's my sister's name. She's in the hospital and I don't know if she's going to get better."

"*Caramba.*" He responded. "Ok, I won't forget. Liliana." He gave me a smile and I left the room for my next class.

I hadn't told Lily yet about the naming; I didn't know how she would feel about it. As she sat in the brown plaid chair looking more and more tired, I quickly spit the story out. "Lily, I picked your name for my Spanish name. I wanted you to know I did it because I was worried about you. Now, I'm Lily too."

She simply looked at me with her tired eyes, and gave a closed-mouth smile. "Ok, Kirsty."

Flying Higher

When bad things happen, the aftermath is first filled with shock. Shock is its own kind of logic. It's a kind of logic in which someone who just experienced a car wreck says the next thing she wants to do is get her driver's license. Shock is an acceptable response, and one accounted for in the way physicians care for patients who have experienced trauma. After the shock for me came lots of questions. Why? Why did this happen to me? I was living along just fine, but suddenly my life was exactly that: *was*.

My first self-proclaimed task was I had to figure out the meaning of life. I had now felt death, so where was this God who claimed us when we died? Who is God? Where is heaven? I remember flying the first time after the accident. I became excited as the plane got higher and higher in the sky. I looked out the window; then felt disappointed.

All those images of heaven as a sunny place with puffy clouds and golden gates, even though I knew it wasn't true, gave me this unconscious hope that just maybe I would see my Dad jumping around in the clouds if the plane just could get high enough. Almost a Delta Silver Medallion Member and I still have yet to see him.

To my dismay and eventual comfort, attempting to answer the questions of my grief is a process; one that changes as I change, and resurfaces at different times depending on new life experience. Even so, at the time, minutes, days, weeks, months, after the car accident, I wanted an answer and I wanted it right now.

Within a few weeks of the car accident, I started high school. I walked into the building with a black letter D on my forehead, one that some people chose to see while others chose to ignore.

My Spanish class watched the movie *Finding Nemo*. At the time, I thought myself perfectly composed, able to face any situation without flinching at the grief triggers, but I was definitely wrong. My mom wrote my teacher requesting that I receive an alternate activity instead of watching the movie with the rest of the class. She said something about "Finding Nemo causing Kirsten to think about Finding Dad."

I thought this was silly, but it worked to excuse me from the assignment. To my surprise, she had success excusing me from assignments several times while I was in high school; there was a movie in history class with lots of blood and guts that I couldn't handle or a school wide assembly addressing the dangers of driving under the influence of alcohol by reenacting an accident scene. Some situations were more jarring to me than others, nevertheless I felt I could play the "Grief" card and get almost anything I wanted. The day my class watched *Finding Nemo* I spent most of the time in the hallway working on something mindless. Eventually, my teacher came out and sat next to me on the floor. I don't know if I remembered at that point, but he was the only one of my new high school teachers that had met my dad. How?

In January, 8 months before our car accident, there had been "8th Grader Night" at the high school. On this evening, we were the high school's patrons. As guests, we were admitted to the lunchroom. The yellow light reflecting off the off-white tiles was as if the room were a living yellowed newspaper clipping wrapping us inside the special attraction: teachers lobbying for why their class was the best.

My mom and I arrived at the beginning and endured countless minutes of socializing with other parents and their too-cool-to-be-here students. Kirsten and the adults again; a familiar chorus for me. The main presentation started and finished before Dad called to say he was on his way. We directed ourselves toward the foyer area where we began to meet teachers, asking about the difference between Honors and Advanced Placement or what Post Secondary Enrollment Option meant. It was almost time for us to leave, and there was still no sight of Dad. I turned around looking for something new to do, when I spotted him. As is classically my father when he is late, he tried to sneak in a back door to slip in the crowd without notice. This time, he entered near the table of the Foreign Languages, and struck up conversation with my future Spanish teacher. I will never forget the image of my dad and my teaching laughing with each other about fishing in the yellow light of the high school cafeteria foyer. Front page of my memory's newspaper.

When Señor Montes came out to meet me that day during *Finding Nemo,* he didn't have a lot to say. He sat down next to me on the floor, and asked:

"What are you thinking about?"

I don't remember what I responded. All I remember is that he listened. He nodded, soaked it all in. When he stood up to return to class, he said:

"If you ever need anything, come talk to me."

At first, I thought, ha. I tricked him. I got him to fall for my sob story and now I can ask for anything I want.

But now, I believe the me that thought this way was the part of me in denial of my grief. I denied that it was something I would need help with. The irony is Señor Montes saw the hurting child, while I, the hurting child, didn't see it in me. As his words echoed in my mind, a tiny part of me also recognized that what he said to me gave me comfort. I had someone who would listen to me in the world of high school, and I don't think I would have made it without him.

At the beginning, I had several other opportunities for exiting high school during the day. For the first few weeks, almost every day I had a different friend of my mom who would offer to take me out to lunch. I almost always returned to my geometry class late, and eventually the teacher and students stopped caring that I was late. Who was it when the door opened halfway through class? That sad girl. I stopped caring too. Slowly, the moms had to return to their daily routines and my lunches dwindled to once a week. My weekly staple.

At school, my counselor, Mrs. Lempke, invited me for weekly lunches with her, which also proved a helpful retreat. We were often chatty enough to similarly facilitate my late arrival to geometry. This left three days a week where I had free time during lunch to attempt conversation with the students who had been my friends in middle school. Some days it went better than others. And on the best days, I could slip into Señor Montes' office and eat lunch with him. All through the lunch conversations, I would survey these adults about the current question on my mind.

"If Jesus is the truth, the way, the light, what happened to all those people who lived before Jesus, and never had the chance to choose him? If God is a loving God, he wouldn't just leave those people behind and outside of his love and grace simply because they were born 10,000 years too soon?"

After school, I saw a counselor at the infamous Mayo Clinic for about 6 months. She lived outside of my social circle, and I had to explain situations to her that my other informal counselors already understood. To a certain extent, walking through stories again for the medical counselor was helpful, but most often I walked away with her encouraging me to let me feel the sadness. I didn't want to feel sad.

On the other hand, my mom didn't let me use sadness as an excuse to stop living. I don't know how my mom knew to push me that way. Somehow she recognized that we had to choose life, a life with support from our community, over the darkness of our pain much earlier than I did.

Even though I had many outlets for my contemplation about life, death, meaning, random plans, four years later in an email to Señor Montes I was still trying to comprehend the meaning of bad things happening in life. I wrote:

"Sometimes I think it is so frustrating that life has to have so many levels. Why can't there just be one? (The deep one)."

Four years out, and my life barely consisted of anything other than the deep level of thinking.

More years later, I walked into work one day and noticed a poster on the wall for the first time which read: *"Cuando hay una tormenta, los pajaritos se esconden pero las águilas vuelan mas alto* [When there's a thunderstorm, the little birds hide, but the eagles fly higher]."

Ding! That's when it hit me.

The thunderstorm comes, it looks different each time although there are certainly patterns, and we decide how to react. Will we be little birds and choose to quickly find an adequate place to hide while the storm passes? Or will we be eagles and fly higher as the storm is about to hit? Will we risk finding a durable place, or will we push ourselves to find the lightness beyond the thunderstorm?

Either way, we can brave the storm, right? But we end up different at the end. As an eagle, I have found my courage, my strength, perseverance, my drive to not let what I can't control dampen what I can be. As the little bird, I recognize when it's better to wait it out, and I risk that the world around me is strong enough to protect me from the storm. We have agency. We choose.

A friend of mine who also survived a traumatic car accident points to a comment from one of his physical therapists that propelled him to choose the effort to regain strength rather than exist forever in a sedentary state.

She said to him, "You may not know it today, you may not know it tomorrow. But there is a reason for what's happened to you."

As much as I find this justification for bad things happening angering, for my friend, this statement gave him hope. Hope that someday he might know something, that someday he could look back and make sense of what happened to him, that someday he could move and live and be unlike the way of the dreary future in which he was unable to walk, run, or even stand that he saw.

What these different moments of choosing the path of life get down to is that each of us had to choose something to keep us going. We had to choose something even what may be an unlikely optimism to give us the capacity to move again. I will not ever be able answer all the questions I have and my friend may never understand why a bad thing happened to him, but the convincing ourselves of an optimistic possibility is the important part. We picked something, something tangible or abstract, that we could get behind and live for despite the storm of questions, confusion, emotion, and challenge that plagued us along the way. Given my dad was an Eagle Scout, I think he'd be proud to know in my family circle, we choose the eagle.

Cars

Choosing to fly higher was the first step. Living by flying higher is an ongoing challenge. It started with the basics, and it didn't take long before that meant facing utter terror. It happened in October on the way to the apple orchard when I sat down in the back seat of the car behind the driver for the first time since the accident.

When we first moved into our house in Rochester, my parents spent a lot of time landscaping. We planted maple trees amidst the forest of buckthorns, apple trees alongside the line of our property, hostas along the pathway to the house and delineated a front garden for shade plants. We created a vegetable garden alongside the back of the house and then doubled the size of the garden the next year, and the best part, we built an above ground pool in the back yard.

With time, the natural elements, children playing in the yard, and young dogs running circles around the house, wore down the landscaping work he had tried to arrange. Life needs maintenance, care, and time to continue as it was. Without the intentional effort to maintain a yard, it will, naturally and on its own, change and become something other than it was. Change is a natural force in life.

Of all the landscaping projects that made our home more our

own, the apple trees became the focus for Dad. He dedicated ingenuity and effort to their wellbeing, creating supports from the wrath of nature and protections from the deer which desired to chew away at the bark. Each fall, we visited an apple orchard outside of town, to pick apples, run through the corn maze, and sample delicious caramels. When Dad saw those apple trees, the desire for our own miniature orchard in the backyard was ignited once more, more insistent than the last time,

After the accident, we chose to move through the moments of shock by attempting to live out what would have been had the change in our family face not happened. We woke one fall morning, and uncle Doug offered to drive us to the apple orchard along the Mississippi river near Pepin, WI. This was the epitome of all apple orchards. As well as I can remember seeing the apples on the trees and walking into the store to purchase the latest and greatest infused cider options, the moment that stands out most from this memory is being in the car.

I pulled open the door of the mud room and walked into the garage.

"I'll drive," Doug said from behind.

"Girls, why doesn't one of you sit in the back?" Mom asked. Allison crawled back without a question. I walked past the driver door, opened the rear door, and sat down behind the driver seat.

Oh no.

Doug opened the driver door, and sat down behind the wheel. I gulped, bracing myself for the inevitable: the engine revving.

I focused on the seat back pocket in front of me, holding the edge and breathing slowly to calm myself down. *Thud thud thud thud thud thud.* My heart pounded.

I sat back into the seat monitoring my breath. I straightened my body to face forward and lifted my head.

Ugh.

From behind, Doug looked as if he were my dad.

Oh no.

Thud thud thud thud thud thud thud.

I tried to focus on the situation at hand. I narrated to myself what was happening. 'Doug is taking us to the apple orchard. Mom is sitting next to him in the front sea-' *whoa.* Doug moved the car in reverse and we pulled out of the garage.

Breathe. Breathe.

I looked up and saw the shape of Doug's head around the head rest, the broad shoulders, hands on the steering wheel, and could only think of the last image I had of Dad, driving in the same way. It was a new moment, but it became a reincarnation of the old moment.

The longer we drove the angrier I became. It was kind of Doug to help us live a joy of my Dad's in visiting the apple trees, but it was wrong. Doug didn't take us to see apples, Dad did.

I felt wrought with worry, certain the car would suddenly explode again, this time with my eyes open to see what happened.

But, it didn't.

As we pulled back into the garage several hours later, I couldn't move. I sat in the seat everything inside me that had become more and more tightly wound slowly releasing. I opened the car door, slammed it behind me, said "Thanks, Doug," opened the mudroom door, walked up the stairs to my room, closed the door calmly behind me, and burst into tears.

Dear Dad,

Why am I so mad? What is wrong with me? I know I need a positive attitude and no one can make me have that, but what is wrong with me? I try to tell Mom but she doesn't like to hear me beat myself down and doesn't like these negative comments. How can I change my attitude? I feel like I am mad at home and I don't want to be. I hate myself because of it and I don't want to be mad around my family. I need Mom and Allison and Lily and Heidi the most right now. I never see them it seems and when I do I am in a bad mood. What can I do to help me? I NEED HELP!

Even Mom told me this morning that I wasn't Kirsten and she knows it. She wants to get rid of this thing that is taking over me. Maybe she feels relieved every time I get on the stupid bus. She doesn't have to deal with me anymore.

Why am I like this?

Nobody else in our family get as mad and so often! Why me? What is wrong with me? Is this what hurt me in the accident?

I know I can't think like this. I have to find something that makes me happy.

I just need help, Dad. What can I do? This is when I really need your guidance. I have your blood; I should try to learn your way of life.

Love with all my heart.
Kirsten

Take it back

The lottery tempts. It tempts us to dream fantasies that only one in many will receive. Even then, there's reason to believe winning the lottery isn't a gift. In a world that runs on flows, the mountain pond grows stagnant and filled with algae when the inlet and outlet streams stop flowing; then the lottery is a curse.

When my dad died, he was the primary income source, primary policyholder; he was actively contributing to the labor force of 21st century United States. My dad's job and ability to provide for us as a family was based on his salary. Without him, the flow stopped.

There are steps we take to protect ourselves from these moments, buying insurance for when the rainy day comes. These steps, though, come in sums. Lump sums. The temptation to see these rainy day precautions as a lottery whispers softly.

When seen all at once, plenty of riches look enormous. Larger than I'd ever seen before. For a moment, it feels warm. And yet, it's from one moment for all time. From this one minute, make it last. Make it last? How do we make it last? The days begin to accumulate. Will there be enough?

Not only that, there's the real life moments that hit as the days accumulate too. I felt as though there were strings attached. Big ones in fact.

Dad wasn't coming home again. I won't ever hear his voice again. He'll never say "Hey, Kirsty girl! What's up?" or even reprimand me for making a choice that disappoints him. He won't show up for my birthday. He won't make it to Christmas this year, or next. He's gone from the homework help. He won't pick me up from dance class again. He'll never be there to give a bear hug when he comes in the door, because he won't come in the door again. He won't cook Sunday evening special dinners, because who knows if time even exists for him. He won't go for a swim in the pool, or pet our dog Bobber until he's asleep. He doesn't know how the next season of 24 is going to end, because he wasn't around to watch last season. As I began the list of things he wouldn't do anymore, I thought, can I change my mind? I don't want this kind of lottery. Take it back.

But with this lottery, by the time I'd experienced a sliver of the life ahead of me, the event, the unspeakable, unhopeable, situation of losing my Dad had already happened. There was no turning back.

Elves

As the days got darker, so did the reality of our new life. Days and weeks passed, and I felt as though it could have been only a matter of minutes or hours. It took an hour for me to take one, good deep breath, and by the time I'd chosen clothes and eaten some food half the daylight was already gone. Everything in my world slowed, except, the world itself did not.

By the time November came along, I remember being shocked one day when the sun set at 4:30pm. When did this happen? Now, the darkness and sadness from inside me was reflected in the long, cold nights of the winter. How could I ever accomplish what I needed to for 9th grade when the darkness surrounded and welcomed me into its embrace nary a few minutes after I left the school building?

During my lunches with Mrs. Lempke, the subject of our conversations touched on my schoolwork in some capacity. I explained how challenging it was for me to move so quickly through material. I could barely keep up. I felt as though I was constantly behind, running to keep up but my mind and body wouldn't move fast enough.

The day after the end of first quarter in November, Mrs. Lempke sat with me as we looked at my grades. I think she was fully prepared for guiding me into remediation and make up assignments, after hearing my weekly stresses feeling incapable of completing my schoolwork.

"What?" she exclaimed as we looked at the report card.

"What?!" she repeated.

"Mrs. Lempke?"

"Kirsten, what are you talking about? Barely being able to keep up with your classwork?"

"What do you mean?" I asked confused.

"The lowest grade you received this quarter was an A-."

"Yes?" I replied.

"You said you were struggling with your school work. An A- is a good grade."

"Mrs. Lempke, you don't understand. I could never get a bad grade. My dad worked very hard to teach me school and grades were important."

"Then, I don't understand. You have very good grades."

"It's not the grades that are challenging. Mrs. Lempke, learning how to get a good grade is a rather simple game. Just because I can earn an A in a class doesn't mean I'm not struggling. How am I supposed to calmly and composedly watch a movie about the French Revolution and see bodies slayed by swords, then take five minutes to switch my brain to make a meaningful comment as the class analyzes *Night* by Eli Wiesel, then move to math, chemistry, Spanish, all within a short matter of time? I can't. It takes so much effort and energy to focus my attention and dedicate myself to one material, and by the time I do so, it's the next class already. It's whiplash. My head doesn't move from one thing to next so quickly right now. Nothing I think about is ever closed or finished. I can't compartmentalize because everything reminds me of something which reminds me of Dad."

She paused and looked at me for a long time. "What can I do to help you?" she asked finally.

"I don't know." I said, starting to tear up. "I don't know."

Later that night, I told my mom about the conversation with

Mrs. Lempke, and she immediately phoned the school to set up a meeting with her. Mom requested that as many of my teachers be made available to attend as well. To this day, I don't know what she said in that meeting, or how my teachers responded. All I know, is that they listened, and brainstormed several ways to help.

"Kirsten, Mr. Brown said you can check out a second history textbook to keep at home so you don't have to carry it back and forth from school."

"Really?" I asked.

"Yes. I thought that might help with the heaviness we feel right now. After he offered, so did all your other teachers. Now, you have a complete set of everything here for you."

At first, I didn't like this accommodation. I thought they were making a special case for me, which they were. But, within a few days, this simple shift alone in how I moved around the school building significantly helped me feel better about school. I didn't have to run around in the few minutes I had after school to collect all the materials I needed before catching the bus which parked farthest away from the building and left the parking lot first every afternoon. My pace had been minorly adjusted for in the pace of the world.

"All your teachers also know now that you are a good student. They said if you ever need extra time on an assignment, or need some space from the class to ask them."

"It's not the assignments that are hard to complete, Mom. It's doing school itself."

"I know, Kirsten, but at least you have a little more flexibility, and now they've seen your grades this first quarter. They trust you."

After Lily came home from the hospital, her activity was limited for a long time. With her blue shell, which covered her torso all the way around, even bending down to tie her shoes was out of the question. No longer did she have any aspiration for dancing, something we all had participated in from when we turned three. In October, she had shown up at the auditions for the younger children wanting to dance in the Nutcracker at Christmas time. Although she couldn't move, we were surprised in November when the youth cast list was posted, and Lily's name appeared first at the top of the page.

Lead Angel: Lily Schowalter

Underneath some thirty other names of youth were listed, but Lily was the only one with a lead part.

"Wow! Lily. How amazing! You're the lead Angel!" I exclaimed excitedly.

"Look at you, Lily! Good job!" chimed Allison.

All around her, Lily received congratulatory remarks, and yet she remained rather placid about the news.

"What do you think, Lily?" I asked her.

"It's good, Kirsten. It's good. It's nice of them to give me a part." She said.

"What do you mean?" I asked.

"Do you really think they gave me that part because I earned it? They gave me the Lead Angel part because I'm the oldest girl that auditioned that day, I can't dance, and they had nowhere else to put me." She replied somberly. "I'm happy I get to participate, but it doesn't feel that good when I know they just felt sorry for me."

That year, Lily was the best darn angel I had ever seen. She had a skirt that skimmed across the floor, as if she were floating rather than walking, and she mastered the tiny steps she needed to take in order to keep it that way. She had a million-dollar smile as she nodded to her angel followers, Clara, and the Sugar Plum fairy, and her blonde hair truly made her look angelic.

Yet watching her on that stage, I realized exactly what she meant when she felt little enthusiasm for playing the part. She felt defeated.

From the moment, she stepped out of the hospital and back into her everyday life context, she had been working so hard to act as normal as possible. As much as she appreciated the director taking into consideration her mobility in casting Lily a role in the Nutcracker, her lead part highlighted her as different from everyone else rather than letting her slide back into a sense of normalcy on the stage. There is nothing wrong with the accommodation Lily received in order to participate. As much as she tried to be optimistic about her recovery, Lily had to accept she actually *needed* the accommodation she was given. She couldn't feel included because she was hurt and unable to dance as another part might have required, and so she was included, but being included also meant that she was pinpointed as being different, she had a special part for the girl who can only walk around and has to wear a blue back brace.

It felt like the world saying, "Yes, Lily it's true. That's all you can do. Nothing but walking and smiling for you." It's a victory and a defeat wrapped up in one.

Making adjustments at school or dance wasn't the only challenge of the darkening days. The darkest time of year is accompanied with the holidays, and for us it was a new season to experience the absence of Dad. Dad loved Christmas. In the past, he spent extra time organizing the holidays so that we would believe in the magic of Santa for one year longer.

The Christmas before our car accident, Mom was injured. She'd cracked a disk in her back and was barely able to sit and stand without severe pain. In the car one evening after dance, Dad told me the truth about Santa.

"Kirsten, you've heard your friends talk about Santa not being real, haven't you?"

"Yeah. Caitlin and I got in an argument last week in science class about it. She said Santa wasn't real, and I told her she was wrong."

"In way, you both are right."

"What? Santa isn't real?" I wilted, devastated at the concession from him.

"Santa is real." He said, my hopes rising. "He's part of every one of us. He is the spirit of Christmas. No, he doesn't visit our house each year, but we are his elves, and we get to share the spirit of Christmas with our family."

I didn't know how to take this. On one hand, it was terribly disappointing the real Santa person didn't exist. How can a story like that be so profoundly woven into the holiday time and this person not be *real*? On the other hand, I could be an elf? I could help be Santa for my sisters?

"Mom and I are usually Santa's elves, but this year she is out of commission. She needs to rest and get better. Will you be an elf with me?" Dad continued.

I paused only for a moment. "Yes! Yes, Dad. I want to be an elf." Dad and I were going to do it together.

Over the next few weeks, Dad taught me where he hid the special Santa wrapping paper. We had special times when he showed me the hiding spot for the Santa gifts behind the washer in the basement laundry room (where my sisters and I were too scared to have ever considered looking). Sometimes I would have a cover story for him while he wrapped gifts, and other times he had a cover story for me. When Christmas Eve finally arrived, I didn't know how it was all going to happen.

"Bed time girls! We can't be awake when Santa gets here. He might skip our house."

"Santaaaaa!" Heidi squealed, running toward bed. Allison and Lily were a little more hesitant.

"Liiilly, I know you are awake over there. You can't trick me into thinking you are asleep on the couch. *Help me Jesus...*" Dad taunted as he walked over to give the feigning Sleeping Beauty a tickle.

"Eeek!" She squealed and soon was awake enough she could not rightfully sleep on the couch while Santa was expected.

As Dad carried her upstairs amidst protest, he called back "You too, Allison! Bedtime."

"I want to see Santa. I'm not going anywhere." Allison demanded. While Dad had already exited the room with Lily, it was my turn to take action. I had to persuade Allison to head to bed with my usually bout of skepticism otherwise she would know something is up.

"Allison," I whispered to her. "Let's go to bed, and we'll wait, quietly awake in bed. Just until Mom and Dad are asleep. Then, we can come down and catch Santa."

"No. I want to wait here. Why do I have to go to bed first?"

"Because Mom and Dad are watching. Plus, Santa always wears bells. Even if we aren't sure whether the coast is clear to come back down, we can know when he's here. We will hear him." I kept my eyes fixed on her, willing her to believe me. Come on, Allison, believe. Believe me. Believe in Santa.

"Ok fine. I'll come get you as soon as I hear something. And you come wake me up too."

"I will. I will." I replied, our plan confirmed.

As soon as this was done, I realized I too would need to go to bed to keep her from being suspicious. But, what was I to do? She would hear me coming downstairs. How could I be an elf and pretend to sleep at the same time? Just as the worry began to cross my face, Allison already turning toward the stairs, I saw Dad coming down. He winked at me. He winked, and I knew I had done a good job and needed to follow through what I told Allison. I climbed the stairs with her, and we went to our separate beds. Dad came in to wish us goodnight and whispered in my ear, "Good job, Kirsty girl. We'll start in a little bit. I'll come get you when it's time." He returned to the top of the stairs and went down to be with Mom.

Everything went off without a hitch. Allison and I fell asleep waiting, and Dad woke me a while later. I crept slowly down the stairs, and while Mom watched and directed from her position in the chair, Dad and I placed each gift and filled each stocking just as I knew Santa did. Dad taped the Santa letter onto the fireplace, and then called me over to him.

"Here, Kirsten. Someone has to eat the cookies." He said.

For a moment, I was shocked. Those were Santa's cookies. I remembered we were the elves, and began to nibble cookie and slurp milk just as I knew Santa liked to do. I left bite marks on a few and ate the rest. After all the bites, I was very full. The job was finished.

The next morning, Christmas felt different. I should have expected it. No longer was I running downstairs in surprise. I knew what everything looked like. No longer were the gifts inside each package unknown, new, exciting. I had wrapped them myself. I felt disappointed by the lack of novelty I felt.

One glance toward Dad, and a new joy entered my heart. No, it wasn't a surprise for me this year, but I got to create the surprise for my sisters and Mom. I had been an elf. Dad and I together.

I couldn't believe the fortuitous situation by the time we approached Christmas after the accident. In many ways, I was not prepared for the responsibilities I confronted and still confront after the accident, but in a few rare situations it was as though Dad had trained me in without either of us knowing he needed to. Christmas and Santa's elf was one of those situations.

"How are we ever going to do Christmas this year?" Mom asked during one of our many dark night conversations. "Your Dad was the master mind of Santa. How can we ever do this?"

Immediately, I too was socked with the devastation that Dad wasn't Santa anymore. Then, it struck me: "Mom, Dad taught me how to be Santa." She looked at me confused for a moment, and then smiled.

"That's right. He did. I forgot my back problem. You were an elf last year, weren't you?"

I smiled. "Yes. I was. We can do this."

As the gifts were purchased, hidden, wrapped, and placed for Christmas that year, I think it went surprisingly well. In addition to my elf help, Mom enlisted my aunt, uncle, and cousins to elf service too. They were crucial members of Santa's team too. Between all of us, Santa came, as usual to our house that Christmas.

What I didn't expect was how much helping as an elf had distracted me from Dad's absence. When the elf work was done, Allison, Lily, Heidi, Mom, and I sat around the tree Christmas morning. Dad's laugh wasn't there. His stocking was empty. There were no gifts for Dad under the tree. Even if we could make Santa come, we couldn't make Dad come back.

That year, we left the Christmas tree up for a long time. I couldn't bear to take down this symbol of a spirit of joy that Dad loved. Being an elf, even without Dad, felt like it brought me close to him for a while. It was a special experience I got to have with him, one I wish every year Allison, Lily, and Heidi could have had.

The phone rings.

"Hello?"

"Hi, I am Christina calling from the American Heart Association. Can we speak to Dave Sckowalter?"

"He's not here."

"Can you tell me a time when he might be available to receive our phone call?"

"No."

"Will he be around later this evening?" Christina prods.

"No."

"Could you give us another time to call back and speak with him?"

"No, he's dead."

Silence.

"I'm sorry for your loss, ma'am." She manages to stutter.

Silence.

"Take care. Have a good night." She ends the conversation.

"Yeah." I say as I hear the other end of the line disconnect.

Itasca

My mom and my dad's oldest brother undertook writing Dad's obituary. I remember them spending hours in front of our computer parsing words. People passed by in search of the shredded turkey sandwiches or baked mac and cheese as Mom and Doug wrote and argued and wrote again, attempting to capture a full, yet shortened, life in a matter of words.

When it was printed, Allison read aloud the first words to us all, "The late Dr. Schowalter... How did the newspaper know Dad was always late?"

Mom turned to Doug, both chuckling.

As Allison continued, the end described us survivors. For this part, Mom had easily filled in the roles my sisters and I had taken on at that moment. They titled me "The Organizer." They titled Lily "The princess." Heidi was "The entertainer," and Allison was: "The comic relief." By saying those words about us, it was as if we had been given roles to fill, roles that at the time felt like a guide, but later have come to feel like clothes too small to wear anymore.

One day, eight years later, a family friend asked me, "How does Allison grieve?"

I didn't have a clear answer. I don't have a specific answer for anyone in my family. Certainly, we share our feelings, we give time and space when possible. The longer I thought about it, the more I remember this label from the obituary: the comic relief.

From my perspective, Allison always seemed so *on*. In the days when I barely left my parents' bedroom, she greeted everyone at the door, welcomed them into our home, thanked them profusely for their gifts and consolation. She jumped back into her school and friends without seemingly a ripple, and I couldn't understand it. She made everything look so simple, and yet she had lost the same Dad I had. That's what I told this friend.

A week later, Allison called me from college and said, "Kirsten, I've been trying to deny it, but I don't think I can any longer. I am grieving Dad again. I am hurting for things I never let myself hurt for. And why would I have? As a 12 year old girl I knew and was told I wasn't injured. I could look at myself and I didn't wear the bandages you did, so if I wasn't hurt, then I wasn't hurt, right? No hurt outside or inside. So sure, I was the comic relief."

I had never heard her speak about herself after the accident like this. She had never told me when she was 12 and grieving she didn't realize she could feel hurt, because she was told she wasn't hurt. Eight years of time, a little bit of crying, and enough triggers like a friend in a car accident, and it forms an equation perfect for reliving raw grief still inside. Why does life do that? Something is always a reminder of Dad: something he did with us, gave us, something he would have enjoyed. We can't forget the people we truly care about, because life is full of reminders.

"I woke up this morning to go to class, and I grabbed my Dansko shoes to wear. They are really cute and comfortable and I wanted to wear them." She told me.

"But as soon as I grabbed them, I remembered the brown high heeled mary jane shoes I loved when I was 10. They had a hole in the heel, and Dad always told me they were perfect, because that was where I could store my bubblegum. 'Everyone needs a heel with a hole so they can store their bubblegum.' He used to tell me. And suddenly my face was wet, covered in tears and I couldn't stand up.

"My Danskos are my bubblegum shoes now. They are the same shoes. I can't wear these, I thought, and then realized I had 15 minutes before I needed to sit composedly in class.

"How ridiculous is that?" She asked. "I started bawling over a pair of shoes. I looked at them and was crying.

"And then I looked up the obituary because I wanted to read it, and it said I was 'the comic relief.' I don't think anyone would call me that anymore. Even my boss who sees me every day would say other things first. 'She's responsible. Reliable. Sure, she has a cute sense of humor.' But I'm not the comic relief."

I chuckled remembering how I felt confused over my label too.

"I started crying again, because it made me think how long it has been since that was me. It's been such a long time. I'm such a different person since then."

She didn't say it, but in that moment I knew she was wondering, 'Does Dad even know who I am anymore?'

"Walking around school now, I feel like I can barely keep my composure. My cover is torn,"

I thought to myself 'It was flaky and fragile to begin with,' knowing mine is exactly the same way. She continued, "and this raw inside is still there. It's still there. Just right here," she pointed to her heart, "and it hurts.

"I've been trying to exercise too, getting into healthy patterns, and each day this week, I catch myself crying as I get to the hardest part of the run. I feel myself wanting to stop, but then I get this incredible fear of stopping. Stopping is giving up, it's not living, it's over, and then I won't make it."

"Have you thought about why that is?" I asked. "That sounds an awful lot like the mantras Mom used to tell us about 'Keep jumping the hoops. Just keep jumping the hoops. No, don't stop.' Have you thought about whether you internalized them so much they are becoming branded into you rather than a helpful strategy for motivating you to keep living?"

"No." She responded quietly. She paused her stream of words to think for a moment. "Yeah." She continued, thinking not sharing.

"The other thing too," She added, "I think anytime something hurts me, or I hear about someone dying, I automatically go back to the hurt that I have about Dad. I think maybe it's because I felt his loss so profoundly that the experience and feelings that go along with it have become the foundation for all my experiences of loss. Everything goes back to Dad. It might not even be about him, like this friend who died in a car accident, but when I start crying or start talking about my hurt, I'm talking about Dad, not my friend."

'How insightful,' I thought, 'It's like Dad is the root, the source, the headwaters of all hurt because he put a face to those emotions and experiences in the deepest way we had ever experienced.'

I recall an image of Dad, Allison, Lily, and I climbing across the rocks at Lake Itasca, the headwaters of the Mississippi River. In the photo, I'm strategizing one foot on one rock the other on a different rock with my pelvis facing where we came from, turning around behind me to gesture with my hands as to which rocks to trace next. Dad has both his feet balancing together on one rock, at the point of utmost precariousness when an object is top heavy and has a small base. Allison is behind Dad focused on each step, and Lily is grabbing Dad's hand as she makes her next move.

Dad is our Itasca. The waters of the Mississippi begin at Itasca and the waters of our grief begin with Dad. Farm Grandma, City Grandpa, other extended family or acquaintances are trickles, streams, or rivers of various sizes increasing our experience of grief at a different location along our journey, and once we reach the ocean we know we will be free, all the waters flowing together in rocking waves of unending distance and time.

"Sometimes I wish I could call him," Allison said, bringing me back from my ocean reverie. "It's funny, because I called Mom and told her I wished I could call Dad, and she responded by saying, 'At least you can call your mom. I can't call my mom. I can only call my dad.' Isn't that interesting?" She probed. "Mom has a Dad to call, but since Farm Grandma died, she doesn't have a mom. And we have a mom to call, but since Dad died we don't have a dad. It's the opposite, but each wishes we had the other's case too."

I didn't have anything to say. Because it's true. Allison hit the nail on the head. We don't have a dad to call and Mom doesn't have a mom to call.

"I just can't believe it's been almost 10 years since dad died and I still am grieving. I guess I will always, because even Mom at age 51 still misses her mom. She still wishes she could pick up the phone and call her."

But she can't call her. We can't call him. We continue living, we remember they aren't here anymore to live with us, and we become sad, hurt, angry, and frustrated. I guess I find it comforting that Dad's memory will never be too far away, and he will always mean something to me. As the Giver says in Lois Lowry's book, "Memories are forever."

House of Bitterness

The years before the car accident, we joined a group of families from our church in Rochester on a trip to Holden Village in the Cascade mountains of Washington. My dad had been hearing about Holden Village since his days as an undergraduate at St. Olaf.

We flew to Seattle, and rented a car, sleeping one night at a hotel in Wenatchee which had bright, red apples free in a bowl in the lobby. Every time I walked past the bowl, I eyed those apples. Feeling a nudge from behind, Dad whispered in my ear, "Kirsten, go grab a couple of those."

With a smirk and a bit of gall, I reached up into the fruit bowl and claimed at least three, depending on the size of the apple, sneaking away to our room, car, or other destination. An apple a day keeps the doctor away.

As we approached the landing where the boat supposedly took us up Lake Chelan to the bus to Holden, two of the staff walked out with a long rope. They tied the rope to either side of the dock, and the sign hanging in the middle read, "Closed due to fire hazard."

No! How could it be that we were so close, on the last leg of the journey, and now the journey stopped?

So it was.

The group met at a small lodge as families made individual choices about how they would spend the time now that their original plans were toast. We spent a pleasant time at the Lodge near Mount Rainier, making ice cream sundaes so big we used a (clean and new) gutter pipe to hold them, hiking just high enough on Rainier so we could see steam coming out the side of the mountain, and watching ever so patiently for whales on the rocks of the San Juan Islands. Although it began with a smash, the week passed in a flash and left great times and fun improvisations in its wake.

One year after the accident, Mom decided it was time to try again. Dad wanted to spend time at Holden Village. Dad felt compelled to be in that space, and it was time for us to journey again. She convinced many of those who were with us the first time to try again travel with us during July to Holden.

We hoped the fires would not keep us away again. Instead of being turned away at the dock, this time we got on the boat, stepped off at the Lucerne landing, and were shuttled to the camp in old school buses on a tiny mountain pass.

It was truly a mountain village like I had never seen before. Crested peaks greeted me each time I walked down the sidewalk on the side of the mountain to pass the chalet on the way to the small valley where the river flowed through the village. I wanted to spend every moment of my time there on the mountain, climbing up and down to find every high place possible.

My mom felt compelled to attend the curriculum designed by the Holden staff, beginning with a Bible study each morning. A pastor gave the study each morning, and with every day the crowds became thicker and thicker. By day three, there were no more seats in the room to sit to hear the words from this pastor.

The first day, he offended my mom. She saw him eating alone in the cafeteria afterward, marched up to him, and argued with him from the next several hours, while 8 year old Heidi climbed on and over the few pieces of furniture in the vicinity.

"How can you say death is not the worst thing that can happen to you? My husband died last year, and I have never experienced anything more terrible than his loss for myself, my daughters, and my family. You try raising four young girls in this world today without a husband, without a full time job."

"I understand you are angry," he replied.

"Angry?! I am more than angry."

"All right, all right, yes. What else are you feeling?" he asked.

"Angry, hurt, frustrated, confused, betrayed, unloved..." listed my mother.

"Yes, and now tell me more. Use those words, build them up around you, they are strong structures, build a house with them. You have every right to. You are hurt, it is not fair. Feel bitter. Be bitter. Yes."

As she continued to speak of the extreme challenge in the world from losing Dad, he finally asked, "Now that you have built this house of bitterness, do you want to live in it?"

M-I-S-S-I-S-S-I-P-P-I

When I was in first grade, we got to choose our own challenge spelling words. One Monday night, Dad had to run back to the Marshfield clinic in order to finish up something from work that day. He asked if I wanted to join him in the car.

As we drove back to the clinic, he said, "Kirsten. Talk to me. Your Pop. What's happening at school this week?"

"I have to pick my challenge spelling words for Friday."

"Did you have a pretest today?"

"Yes."

"How did it go?"

"I got all the words correct on my pretest. That's why I need to pick challenge words."

"What about Mississippi?"

"Daaad. M-i-s-s-i-s-s-i-p-p-i. I know how to spell that word already."

"Um, what about Tuesday?"

"We already did the days of the week last month on our spelling list."

Pulling into the parking lot of clinic, he turned his head toward the building; the name St. Joseph's Hospital was plastered on the wall. "How about hospital?"

"Hospital? How do you spell that?"

"Look, it's right there on the wall. H-o-s-p-i-t-a-l. There. You focus on learning how to spell hospital, while I run inside lickety split to get this sample off the machine, ok?"

Sitting in the car by myself, I spelled hospital to myself several times. H-o-s-p-i-t-a-l. H-o-s-p-i-t-a-l. Hospital.

I saw Dad walking back toward the car through the windshield.

"How do you spell hospital, Kirsten?" he asked as he opened the driver side door.

"H-o-s-p-i-t-a-l."

"Perfect. Let's have a perfect spelling test again on Friday with your challenge words, all righty roo?"

Four days later, Dad walked into the house after work. I averted my gaze from him, and continued to shuffle through the first grade homework papers laying around my feet.

"Hey! Who's the spelling word champion this week?"

I continued to look down at my papers without responding.

"Kirsty, how'd it go?" he prodded.

I slowly lifted a long skinny sheet of paper that said *Spelling Test* across the top and my handwriting scrawled on 15 lines down the page. There was one red circle around a word at the bottom of the page. Hospital.

"Kirsten, what happened?" He asked, pulling the page closer to look at it in more detail.

"I got hospital wrong."

"How?" He asked gently.

"I wrote h-o-p-s-i-t-a-l. I messed it up."

"Kirsty girl! Look at that! You messed it up. How is it supposed to be?"

"H-o-s-p-i-t-a-l."

"See, don't worry. You know how to spell it. You just made a little mistake. You'll never forget it again!" He chuckled, and gave me a kiss on the cheek.

Dishes

I hated doing the dishes growing up. As the oldest child, I learned quickly that my parents parented by using me as the example for my younger sisters; monkey see, monkey do. As such, dishes duty fell to me first to learn how to do correctly and efficiently.

In our house, we operate under the unspoken rule that whoever cooks doesn't clean. Being that Dad often barely made it home before dinner, he was consistently the dishes-doer, while Mom cooked.

"Girls, come set the table!" Mom called as the spaghetti finished. Allison and I came into the kitchen to grab plates, fork, and cups, slamming them onto the table with as little effort as possible.

Just as we sat down in our spots, one "big" girl and one "little" girl on each side of the table, we could hear the sound of the garage door opening. With the final chimes of the Nightly News music fading into the background, Dad entered the house, and k-klopped his way to the kitchen.

"Daddy!" We screamed and ran to him.

"Girls, sit down! We are eating!" Mom scolded, and Dad sat down at the head of the table to join us just in time for the meal.

After sufficient "Allison, you do not need thirds," and

"Heidi, you need to eat your peas," each person brought their plate, fork, and cup, around the counter to the dishwasher. Once all the plates were cleared, Dad began the dishes. I skittered after my sisters, yelling, "I have to go to the bathroom," behind me.

Just as I got around the corner, I heard, *"Kiiirsten*, get back here and help with the dishes."

I was caught red handed.

I slumped back to the dishwasher following Dad's orders.

"Put the cups in line on the top shelf...No! You have to dump the milk out first before putting it in! Now we have to wipe down the cupboards and floors from the spill."

As I continued to randomly place items in the dishwasher, Dad began to wash by hand the larger pans or bowls that didn't fit. He looked over his right shoulder at me working with the dishwasher, "Kirsten, put similar things together. You would have much more space in the bottom if you just line up all the plates next to each other."

After listening to his dish-doing-harping, the job was done. I escaped and resumed playing, forgetting that I had even thought about a bathroom stop only minutes earlier.

Although at first it bothered me that I had to consistently do the dishes with Dad, unlike my little sisters, eventually it became a brief moment in the day that was just the two of us. We worked thoughtlessly and chatted about what we were thinking about or feeling. We even got to the point where we would encourage my sisters and Mom to leave their dishes behind because we had a mutually enjoyable routine.

For weeks after the accident, I wouldn't let anyone near the dishwasher after a meal. They cleared their plates from the table, left them on the counter, and I demanded they leave the kitchen and me alone in it. After all the movement stopped, I would begin the routine, *our* routine. Rinsing each plate, putting it in a neat line, organizing the odd shaped cookware like Tetris into the dishwasher listening to a new soundtrack: silence.

Living through daily moments of grief like doing the dishes quantifies the hurt. Yes, it is a big loss from the start. But only after years, day in day out of getting hit with sadness as I began to move through my old life in a new state of being did I realize how big the loss actually was, how much I held onto because I thought it made sense or would keep me closer to Dad. Facing those surprises every day…that is more overwhelming than I could have ever estimated.

Let go

Nine years later, I left work, got in my car, and pulled out of the driveway in front of a police car. The police car rode up beside me trying to get my attention, then swerved behind and flashed his lights. Within a few blocks, I pulled over. My hands shook nervously as the officer approached my car.

"I need to see your identification, insurance, and vehicle registration."

I reached my hand out the window. He grabbed the papers from my hand, and walked back to his car.

Breathe.

I tried to remain calm as I heard footsteps coming back in my direction.

"You still living up on Viewmont Lane?"

"Yes."

"I'll let you off with a warning this time. Next time, don't pull out in front of another car without more space."

"But it's a blind intersection!" I wanted to retort, "Have you ever tried to make a right turn out of that driveway?"

I held my cool.

"Ok, thank you."

Within minutes, I was on the verge of an emotional breakdown.

"What's wrong with you, Kirsten?" I chided. "Sure, this was the first time I have been pulled over, but that happens to people every day. It's practically a joke for some people."

In the months after our car accident, my mom spent many hours with lawyers working to figure out a settlement and the insurance costs for our car accident. She expressed to me over and over again the awe and frustration she felt about Dad receiving the fault for the accident he was killed in.

"What do they want from us? The man they say is at fault DIED in that accident. He has nothing left, and yet they want more from him? He had a perfect driving record. This was the first time anything had happened to him in the car. How can they call him a bad person? He was a good person and didn't mean to harm anyone. It wasn't his fault."

We processed the information from the police and lawyer reports on a constant replay. 'He had a perfect driving record.' 'He wouldn't hurt anyone,' echoed in my mind.

Seeing as this legal process began and lasted for years, my 16th birthday quickly approached in the midst of this, and I began to drive. I suddenly became an active parent. I coordinated rides for my sisters, I bought groceries, took care of errands, and all of it more than I ever had because of my access to wheels.

I had been preparing for the day I could legally drive from the moments after the reality of the car accident hit me. If Dad had a perfect driving record, I decided I would try for a perfect driving record at least until I was 18. I needed to earn my mother's trust to be able to serve as the second-in-command.

How was I going to measure the goal of a perfect driving record? I was not going to get pulled over.

I was a careful driver. I loved driving because it was the first experience I had after the accident in which my mind and body were totally devoted to a single occupation. My mind wasn't running at speed previously unknown to humankind, my body wasn't sitting restlessly while my mind ran. I was fully engaged and present, and it was refreshing.

Then, like many drivers, I began to acclimate to the practice and the time became filled with other things. My mind didn't need to focus fully on the driving anymore and it became like any other moment in the day, full speed ahead processing of who-knows-what. By the time I turned 18, I realized I had achieved my goal. I had never been pulled over.

Since I achieved my old goal, I decided it was time to set another goal. In this case, the easiest way to set a new goal seemed to extend the goal.

"How about another year of a perfect driving record? Ok." I decided.

So it went. Until somewhere along the line, I decided not to extend the goal for only the next year. No. I thought goals should be continually bigger and better to keep stretching myself. And suddenly, somewhere deep inside me accepted the goal that I would have a perfect driving record forever.

Being pulled over at the age of 22, spurred the impossibility of achieving that goal.

I'm not perfect.

I'm not like Dad.

I'm not the good person he was.

I failed.

I failed him.

I am a failure.

The words zoomed through my head as if these negative self thoughts had been waiting for the opportunity to pounce for ages.

Before my self-esteem could plummet too far, the words of a mentor passed through my head.

"You know, Kirsten, sometimes I think you have created expectations for yourself that are based on something your Dad would have wanted, but that actually cause you to behave and treat yourself in a way far from what he actually wanted for you."

What? What does that even mean?

Rather than brushing off my fleeting experience with a policeman, it became corroborative evidence for my inevitable failure in the face of the standard of success I held myself to. Perfectionism, in other words, had become chiseled into the core of my being. I am not living up to the standard and have disappointed myself from one opportunity to continue to live out Dad's memory. With his memory affirming his success in achieving perfection, I had come to associate what I thought was his standard of goodness as perfection itself.

"I just don't think something your dad did or would expect of you, should be hurtful to you," my friend said to me.

How could anyone else possibly know what my Dad wanted for me?

Oh.

Then, it was clear.

The things my Dad wanted for me anyone could read on his face. He wanted life and joy. He wanted my sisters and I to feel loved and cared for. He wanted us to know we were valued and individual. Yes, he wanted us to be "good" people, but he loved us and what he wanted for us grew out of love. He wanted me to be considerate and caring of other people. Certainly, that means driving carefully so that I don't hurt someone, but he could care less about how many times I got pulled over.

Most importantly, he would not want me to say I was a failure.

He would laugh at me for feeling badly about a minor situation that I did my best to respond to in a positive way, give me a kiss on the cheek, and move on. Just like when I was young and spelled hospital wrong on my spelling test. I would continue to be me, and he would continue to know that I am a good person, not a failure.

It's strange how a memory or a commitment to someone I care about can inspire hurtful self thought. It's a great paradox. I know trying to take care of my family, trying to be perfect just like my Dad is just a cover, a tactic, an unrealistic one at that. I know that's not how it really happened. I know getting pulled over for making a risky turn doesn't make me a failure. But do I know that deep down inside? Apparently not. I'm still learning how to pull apart those deeply twisted tactics inside me to let me live free.

The greatest strength and weakness of humankind is that we

learn from the past. It's a strength because I learn from my mistakes, but it is a weakness because sometimes it holds me back.

Ich Habe Eine Grosse Familie

Spring of my sophomore year of high school, Heidi had a good friend whose family was hosting a foreign exchange student from Belgium. Heidi had spent a fair amount of time with her as she went for play dates to her friend's house.

One evening at home while Heidi and Mom were talking in the family room, Heidi asked, "Can we have a foreign exchange student?"

By the time I returned from dance that evening, Mom was convinced it would be a wonderful idea.

We had spent 20 some months already with a hole at the foot of our family table each night at dinner. We had spent 20 some months realizing how sad it made us every time we opened a prepackaged food that was meant for 6 and there would be one left over. We had spent 20 some months without our Dad, our 6th person, and it felt like a wonderful idea to welcome someone back into our family again.

Loss is hard, but it's clear that for our family welcoming another person, even when we knew we would have to let her return to her own life, was a worthwhile experience. Thinking back on it now, we let ourselves back into the pattern of addition and subtraction in so our lives weren't limited to our experience losing our dad. Subtraction could happen in many ways, in many forms. So, my family grew.

Her name was Marta Quintanilla. She was from Medellín, Colombia. She was 17 years old and her birthday was March 25. Just like Dad's.

My mom and Heidi picked Marta up from the local airport, she sauntered out from behind security, *bajita y morena,* short and dark haired. "She was so beautiful," was all my mom can say about the memory.

"The conversation in the car was so *awkward,*" Heidi claimed, recalling the ride through the snow-covered plains of a Minnesota January to our house. "The moment Marta got out of the car, she stuck her bare hand entirely in the snow." Heidi smirked. "She left it there for a moment, and pulled it out sharply, saying 'Ouch! Snow hurts!'" laughed Heidi as she told me about it.

After a moment in our living room with my mom and I, Marta ran downstairs, dragging me along with her to her suitcases in the basement bedroom. She rummaged through her belongings and began pulling out bracelets, rings, and necklaces. She showed me one after another, colorful and bold, typical of Colombia I now love, but at the time much different than I'd ever seen.

"What are these, Marta?" I asked.

"They are for you." She replied matter-of-factly.

"You mean they are for all my family?"

"Yes. This one, I know, it's…*cómo se dice? La bandera?*"

"The flag?" I responded.

"Yes, of the gay people here, but it's not like that in Colombia. Everybody wears rainbow in Colombia. I hope you like it."

"It's beautiful!" I responded emphatically, smiling at her thoughtfulness.

"Come on, let's take them upstairs and show my mom and sisters. They are gifts for them too."

"Yes, ok," she said. I bolted up the stairs as she called "*Wait!*"

from behind. That would be a recurring problem for her in the U.S., *bajita y morena.*

While Marta was in our house, I had a habit of baking. All the time. Sunday night, 8pm: I baked. Monday after school: I baked. Wednesday before Confirmation class: more baking. Mostly, I would bake the same thing every time: Betty Crocker's Homemade Cocoa Brownies with chocolate chips.

From when I was young, these brownies were my specialty. The 9 x 11 baking pan was hardly clean I used it so often for brownies. I baked anytime I had stress or feelings I didn't know how to handle, so the quantity of brownies in our house was never low.

Marta, happened to love chocolate, so at first this turned out to be a really good deal for her. Until a few months when she stood on the scale and had a rude awakening as to how many brownies she had *actually* consumed during her first few weeks with us. It got to the point where after eating dinner or a brownie or cheesy chips (tortilla chips topped with melted cheddar cheese), Marta would begin to complain how full she was... in terms of babies.

"Oh Kirsty, I can't eat another brownie tonight. Do you know how many babies I already have today? Like 50. I can't eat any more brownies today."

"Marta, I have 150 babies." Allison would tease in response.

"Well, now that I think it, I think I have 200 babies, actually. Actually, yes 200." Marta retorted.

Two hours later... "Kirsty, where are the brownies? I thought we still had some left?"

Oh baby! It became the talk of the house, and even the lunch table at school. The looks we got were pretty hilarious to say the least.

As much as Marta joked with me about the baking habit, I'm glad she bore the responsibility of having to consume the products made. A moment of thoughtless movement in the kitchen saved me many crazed breakdowns, even though there were plenty released too during this time.

When Marta was with us, we were so high on life we got a new puppy. I was 9 when my parents let us get our first dog, Bobber. We drove up to my Uncle Matt's house on May 5, Heidi's 2nd birthday as promised, to pick out Bobber, the grunt of the litter, as Lily called him. We named him Air Bobber Grunt, after Air Bud in the movie series.

At the same time, Farm Grandpa came to pick out one of Bobber's sisters, Bonnie, to live with him on the farm and we took two other sisters, Reba and Cider, to live with Aunt Carol and Uncle Doug. The whole puppy family was going to live with my family.

Even though I wanted a puppy. Bobber was Dad's dog. He was a boy, just like Dad. He was named after a fishing bobber, just like Dad wanted. When Dad was home at night reading the day's paper, Bobber sat next to him. Dad pet him on the head until he fell asleep.

When Marta lived with us, we couldn't imagine losing Dad's dog too after two years without dad. Bobber was in good health, but we still worried what life would be like after him. Our last connection with Dad would be gone, and we didn't need any more emptiness in our house. Imagining walking past the makeshift garage kennel that Dad built with some 2 x 4s and chicken wire without Bobber in it was a pain too acute for us to be anything we were willing to let happen.

"Mom, Carol is getting a new dog from Uncle Matt. I think we need to get one too." said Heidi. With hardly any argument, Mom agreed. A few weeks later, Sunny Jig joined our family.

Inviting Marta and Jig into our house was choosing to make new memories. With Marta, we had something to give for the first time in a long time. We weren't just receiving from others; we could give to her. With Marta, we weren't alone as people who couldn't articulate the experiences we had with the words at our disposal. With Marta, we weren't the only ones experiencing new smells, tastes, places, and faces every day. We weren't the only ones with seemingly overwhelming tasks to complete in order to survive from one day to the next. We weren't the only ones that missed the comfort and familiarity of a home that was no longer the present. Marta was a balm, even temporary as it was.

The day we took Marta to the airport was a heavy day. Allison, Lily, Heidi, and I packed into the back of the Highlander along with Marta's suitcases. Marta slid into the passenger seat, and Mom sat down behind the wheel. We chatted in the car as if we didn't know the destination of the drive, pretending this wasn't the last time we would ride together, laughing and teasing one another. As soon as the large box stores faded into the distance and the scenery outside the window become cornfields, the airport was approaching. Even as we pulled Marta's bags out of the car, rolled them with her over the pedestrian crossing, and moved through the smoothly automated sliding doors, we denied what was happening. Only after Marta checked her backs at the ticket counter and we sat down in some chairs just in front of security did we all become silent facing the truth. We didn't have anything to say. Looking from one to another we all didn't want to say or do what we knew had to come: good bye.

We watched her walk through the security gates, waved as she turned around the corner, and walked back out to the car slowly.

"Let's do that again!"

Three months later, Lea from Milano, Italy came to stay with us.

Lea was contemplative. She had a poster of Ganesha in her room, and practiced meditation and yoga in her free time. She was an artist, and wanted to study psychology. She also was an avid downhill skier. Who wouldn't be when your family owns the best ski resort in the Northern Italian Alps? This time though, not only were we creating new memories and meeting new people beyond the world of our previous history, I also learned a fair amount about independence from Lea. She ventured to do what I would have never done at my high school.

Heidi remembers Lea as our healer. Her space in the basement was like a safe place where any of us could go when we needed comfort. Heidi remembers walking into Lea's room one day and crying on the spot. Lea sat her down on the bed and held her, cooing softly the whole time. I remember sneaking down late at night when Lea would watch TV shows on her laptop. She said, "Hi Kirsty," and I knew I could come in. No matter what she always let me in. She paused her computer, and asked "How are you?" Sometimes I didn't have anything to say, so we resumed watching her show together. Other times, I had plenty to say, and she nodded and listened as I got my frustrations with high school dances or math class off my chest.

New with Lea was that she would be celebrating Christmas with us. Marta came in January, and so the holidays were not part of her time in the U.S. Lea came in September though, and stayed until May. She would get to spend Christmas with us, for better or for worse. What were we going to do?

The first year after the accident, we tried to make the holiday as similar as possible to the past. The second year and third years demonstrated how unhelpful trying to resurrect a dead memory was. Not only was Dad's presence gone, but also the priorities for how we ought to spend our money, if we should even spend it at all, on gifts for the family. Once, I thought Mom might find it more meaningful that I had made a year-end donation to an organization that worked in Costa Rica rather than purchase her something, but on Christmas day the resounding sigh, "Thank you, Kirsten," didn't change the fact that her husband wasn't celebrating Christmas with his daughters. It didn't matter, material or immaterial, Christmas wasn't working for us.

The fourth year Lea was with us. We wanted to do something new. We decided to only give and receive gifts that we had made with our own hands.

Initially, I was scared by the idea, 'How could anything I make meet the standard of a Christmas present?' but it didn't take long before I realized the opportunity of the new rule. Excitedly, I spent a half day during mid October to spread my supplies and gift ideas across our kitchen table and make each gift, one by one, with joy that I had not known was inside me.

"Kirsty, what do you think about this idea for the Christmas gifts?" Lea asked my one afternoon while working on homework. "I want to make something special for my American family."

"That's beautiful, Lea" I answered leaning behind her laptop too look at the image she showed me.

"Do you think it's ok if my mom sends us gifts from Italy too? She wants to send you something for being my family here too."

"Of course! That sounds exciting!" The anticipation grew as the holidays approached. Had anyone seen Allison make anything yet? What did Mom spend so many hours in her bedroom working on?

Opening the gifts on Christmas Day, each of us seemed as though there was an extra warm, golden ball of energy inside that had never be a part of our holidays before. We were *proud* of what we had accomplished and *looked forward* to sharing those accomplishments with each other. Since when did we have motivation for something? Since then.

Lily unveiled the homemade perfume she mixed for each of us. Allison had purchased fleece and created tie blankets. Heidi exercised the budding journalist in her and wrote a story starring each of us as the main character personalized to our interests. I made placards with inspirational quotes in calligraphy handwriting, and Mom used Dad's old shirts to make multicolored teddy bears. Lea's gifts were perfect too. She had crocheted new hats in different color for each of us. It was beautiful.

Of all the gifts, the teddy bears were by far the most challenging for me to receive. The rest of us had created something from new materials, while Mom had intentionally sought a way to make Dad's old shirts into something each of us could keep. Seeing his shirts form the skin of a new, soft, hug-friendly bear was one more step in facing the reality that those shirts were never going to be worn again. The conversation between me and my conscience went something like this:

"How can we make bears out of Dad's shirts?" I wondered.

"Who was going to wear those shirts anyway, Kirsten?" My conscience countered.

"Dad, of course." I replied.

"Uh...Kirsten...um... yeah. Do you remember what year it is? Yeah...um...it's 2010...and well... Your dad... he's dead. He died. In 2007."

Gulp. Shit. Oh no.

"My dad... is dead? Really?" I stammered. "*Really?*"

My conscience sighed knowing it once again was the bearer of bad news; news that tore my heart, mind, and soul apart every time. "Yeah." It said. "I'm sorry."

Both of us knew what happened after that. Here it comes. WHAM. Torrential rain of sadness and desperation. Like I walked into a brick wall. For the hundredth time. This week. With the wind knocked out of me, gone is any reason for continuing to live.

"Walk, Kirsten. Speak. Listen. Breathe." My conscience commanded, and eventually I was minimally conscious of where I was and what I was doing, instead of utterly unaware. That's the best I could ask for.

Honestly, it's a lot of work coming to terms with the same hurt over and over again. After a while, I can finally say to my hurt: "Yes, fine, you are a part of the reason why things are as they are. I will begrudgingly let you into the conversation, because I have no other choice. The mechanisms of life appointed you to a seat at the table of my internal board of directors; I did not elect you. But, I can't change the fact that you have been appointed so I will let you take a seat where you now belong, part of me and my story forever." Scars tell the stories of our lives.

September of the following year, Amie from Wavre, Belgium came to stay with us. If Lea had helped us feel steady, come to terms with our story again, Amie brought humor back into our lives. Lily and Amie could laugh so much they were rolling on the floor with stomachs hurting.

She wasn't particularly religious, and like Marta and Lea before her, she protested when Mom required she attend church with our family. Once, after the cross country season ended, she rode the bus home for the first time alone. She nonchalantly got on the bus and took her seat. Soon enough, she realized she had missed her stop! As soon as the bus made the next stop, she ran off. The bus driver pulled just around the corner before stopping the bus, opening the doors, and yelling out to her, "This isn't your stop, is it?"

Embarrassed and looking for any excuse possible, she yelled back, "Yes, of course it is!...I'm going to church!" pointing at the building which happened to be behind her.

Before the bus driver could respond, she turned around and walked to the front doors of the church, pulling to open one and found it was locked. The whole bus watched as she sulked back, and the bus driver offered to take her back to her stop as he made his way around the block.

While we hosted Amie, Marta convinced us to visit her and her family in Colombia. It was incredible. I have left part of my heart in Colombia. As the trip drew closer, Mom became more aware with each day that many people thought Colombia was unsafe. Why would you take your children to visit *Colombia*? "Because Marta is there waiting for us," she kept telling herself, although it did little to calm her fears.

Spending Christmas on the farm with Marta's family felt so similar to Christmas with my mom's family, we were shocked. It felt so homey. Familiar. Welcoming. Safe. We loved it. That's when we realized our family didn't have to be afraid of the world. Sure, bad things happen, but the beauty of the world is worth fighting for, and each of our exchange student families now are like another part of our extended family. We've spent a Christmas with each of their families' now. Their home is our home. We are one, and ready for new adventure.

The One Who Started it All

After our lives returned to a relative rhythm, Mom became increasingly dissatisfied with her work. She was not intellectually stimulated anymore, and she felt as though the years she spent in her lab work was really a choice she made to support my father's career choice and the well being of my family. She went from a physician's spouse and mother to a single person, remembering the dreams and aspirations she had as a young woman living in Rochester, MN. The most obvious one: she wanted to be a doctor.

This was ridiculous. Absurd. Brilliant. Irresponsible. Crazy. Any adjective, and I can guarantee my mom had thought about it. She thought and thought and read one medical book after another trying to understand this yearning she felt. How was she supposed to quit her job and go back to school? She was a widow, her children young. She was barely keeping up with Parent Teacher Association, Dancing Mom Volunteering, and making dinner at a reasonable hour as it was. But what was the point?

She liked her job before because she got to do science. As the years passed, more of the work was completed by shiny new machines, and her only function was to make sure they were loaded and unloaded properly. It didn't intrigue her, and like mother like daughter, she had too much running around in her head to find babysitting the computer enjoyable. What was the point? Why did this happen to her? What choice did she have?

To start small. That was her choice. Maybe just a class. Online.

"I think I could handle that." She told Lea and I one evening. "There's this Bioethics Master's program online through Loyola, and as long as I'm still working with Mayo Clinic they will pay for the class. It'll give me something to read. I haven't been in college in so long, I don't even know if I remember how to learn," trying to convince herself more than us.

"Sure, Mom. Why not? Can you read this English paper for typos?" I responded.

Soon enough conversations about organ transplant, in vitro fertilization, and Do Not Resuscitate signatures became dinner conversations.

"What do you think girls? Would you want me to sign one of these forms if I had to have a risky surgery? Heidi, I said you need to eat at least 3 of the green beans."

At the end of the first semester, she had to write a paper.

"Kirsten, will you read my paper?"

"Sure."

"What's the question you are answering?"

"It's right here about organ donation."

"You don't even talk about organ donation until 3 pages in."

"Yes, but we talked about Kant in our class, and I'm trying to show how his idea here is part of the conversation…"

"Mom, it's not so clear. I think we need to reorganize a little."

"I've been reorganizing. This is the third time I've tried to write this essay. Maybe I can't do this."

"What if we put this part about organ donation requests on driver's license later?"

"Ok, fine."

"Mom, I know you've been working hard on this. I want you to do well, and you can do it."

"Kirsten, I have too many ideas and don't know how to say them clearly."

This was just the beginning. With each successive class, there was a longer paper. It became routine.

"Kirsten, can you please set aside two hours this weekend. I know, I know, but I need you to help me," she asked as I gave her a look of annoyance. I wanted her to do well, I did, but it felt like an extra burden. Did I need more burdens? Wasn't I doing enough for our family?

"Do you have a draft written?" I asked.

"I've been working on this paper for two weeks now,"

"Ok, Mom. We can do it on Sunday."

As more classes asked for writing, she began gravitating back to the science she knew and loved. One day she came home with a Medical College Admission Test (MCAT) study book.

"I signed up for the MCAT girls."

"You did?" I asked.

"Wow!" Lily said.

"When are you going to take it?" Allison wanted to know.

"In a few months," she said, "For now, I have this book to help me study."

"Do you have to study a lot?" Heidi asked.

"I think so." Mom said.

A few months later, "Girls. I signed up for an MCAT study course."

"What happened?" Allison asked.

"I got my score back, and it's not good enough."

"It's ok, Mommy!" Lily cheered.

"Well, I'm going to try again." She said.

The next week she left one evening for her review course at the local community college.

"Kirsten, I'll be back in a few hours."

"Ok, Mom."

When the door slammed on her return, she had not even entered the living room when we heard, "You'll never believe what happened."

"What?" Allison prodded.

"The teacher of the class,"

"Yes?" I asked.

"He was your Dad's student."

"What?"

"He started at the beginning and did roll call, and came to my name. He looked up at me and said 'Schowalter? As in Dave Schowalter?' I couldn't believe it. 'I'm so sorry for your loss. Your husband was the most amazing teacher. What are you doing here?' I told him thank you and that now I was trying to go to medical school. 'I'm going to do whatever I can to help you. Just tell me what you need.'"

"Wow," Lily responded.

"How can that not be a sign? Your Dad is still here. He's still shaping our lives. What are the chances?"

This time her score was good enough. This time, we all thought, she would get in. We worked on the essays, we helped her with the application, and we were all disappointed when she wasn't accepted to the medical school in town.

"Try getting some different letters of recommendation. Why not look at some Osteopathic Medical schools too?" one colleague advised.

"What about trying the MCAT one more time? See if you can't bump up your score just a little more?" another thought.

"Maybe apply to more than the school in town. Widen your pool a little just so you have some more feedback," said another.

Mom's response? She did all three.

She had tasted a challenge and wasn't going to accept defeat until she had done everything she could. Three years and six months after she first started her bioethics degree, one thing, just one thing changed everything.

Invited

Mom checked her email for the first time after we returned from visiting Marta's family in Colombia on January 5, 2012. There was correspondence from Pacific Northwest University of Health Sciences College of Osteopathic Medicine.

"Dear Karen, We would like to invite you for an interview for the 2016 class of Doctor of Osteopathic Medicine students with PNWU on …"

She got an interview! She got an INTERVIEW! For the first time since she began this process of going back and doing what she wanted for her own life, she *finally* heard an answer other than a flat "no." Someone wanted to talk to her. And not just someone, a *medical school* wanted to interview her for a position.

"Moooommmmm! This is so exciting!" we squealed simultaneously.

"Calm down, girls, it doesn't mean anything. It's just an interview." she responded. "I can't believe they offered me an interview…" she mouthed, exuding awe from every pore of her being. "It must be a fluke. Everyone else so far has said 'no'."

Two days later, she heard another "yes." Two medical schools wanted to interview her. TWO. Not just one, TWO.

"Mom, this isn't a fluke. They want to interview you. They want to know you." Immediately, she disciplined herself to begin preparation work. She had four weeks to review interview procedures and prepare for the various scenarios she might encounter in the process. One weekend, Mom, Allison, Lily, and Heidi visited me in Northfield during the preparation weeks. I had started college at my dad's alma mater a few months before. I didn't know if I loved the freedom I had when it seemed like life at home was getting more exciting since I had left. It made me begin to wonder how much of the darkness I felt inside came from within and not external responsibility or burdens I thought I had to shoulder.

Somehow, we ended up perusing the store fronts downtown and found a consignment shop. Allison and I, thrilled at the notion of purchasing new second-hand clothes, dove into the store, covering every inch of the premise looking for good deals. In one area, there were suits for women.

"Mom, what are you going to wear for your interviews?" I asked.

"I have a couple different suit jackets at home that I can wear." She responded curtly.

"Like what?" I pressed.

"You remember, that green one with the shoulders like this," and she motioned the size of shoulder pads that were part of the suit. "And that colorful one, it goes with a dress skirt. I wear it with my old pumps. You know what I'm talking about, right?"

"Try this." I said. "I think you need something new."

"Kirsten, I have perfectly good suits at home. I do not need to spend more money on these interviews than I already am with flights, hotels, and rental cars…"

"Mom. Try it."

And so, it commenced. We made her try on every updated version of a woman's pant suit in the consignment shop. There were plaid, and black, navy blue, and khaki options. Then, we found it. It was an elegantly tailored dark gray suit that fit her well.

At first, she didn't have much to say about it. She looked at herself in the mirror. She spun around looking how the suit fit from as many angles as possible.

"Why don't you try to walk around in it," the lady working at the counter suggested. Mom meandered through the racks of clothing wearing the suit.

"Just imagine it with a blouse, a solid colored blouse, that will just pop." Allison commented. I ran through the racks in search of a blouse to help visualize the perfection of the suit. I found a red one. Meh, I thought, and brought it for her to try.

"Put this on too." I requested.

"Red isn't my color," she quipped.

"But it will help you see what this suit could look like." I piped back, and Mom acquiesced.

When Mom came back out of the fitting room, Allison said, "Boom, That's it. That's the suit you are going to wear to your interviews."

"But girls, I don't understand why you think I need a new suit. I have perfectly good suits at home."

"Mom. Listen. You are going for medical school interviews. You are a non-traditional student. You can't wear a suit you purchased for your first professional job in the 1980s. You will not come off as a qualified, forward thinking individual if you do that. We want you to look good, and feel good." I said.

"Mom. I am not going to the interviews with you if you are wearing shoulder pads. It is not happening." Allison added, teasing her to emphasize our point.

"You don't think shoulder pads are professional?" Mom joked before admitting, "All right, you have a point. How much is the suit?"

"That's the even better part, Mom. It's a good deal. $50 for slacks and jacket. That's a good price." Allison urged.

"That's $50 you could spend on textbooks, Kirsten," Mom countered.

"No." I said. "You need this suit."

A few minutes later, we stood in front of the cash register making our purchase.

"Now, all you have to do is find a nice blouse," the checkout lady said.

"That's true. There has to be something at Macy's or

JCPenney I could find for a reasonable price." Mom answered.

By the next week, Mom had found a blue blouse from Macy's that made her eyes pop and she was ready. It was time to interview.

Allison was Mom's companion on the interview trips, one to Maine and the other to Washington, because she would be a senior in high school for Mom's first year of medical school, were Mom to be accepted.

"Allison, I want you to tell me what you think of these places. You have to check out the towns for me."

For the PNWU interview, the school arranged for Allison to visit the nearest high school during the day while Mom interviewed. Walking into East Valley High School was a shock to the system for her. With a student population majority Hispanic, Spanish spoken in every hallway, and only two Advanced Placement classes, this was clearly not our home of Rochester, MN with highly educated physicians and their high-achieving children. Driving around Yakima with the wife of a current student, Allison asked "Do you shop often at the Walmart nearby?"

"No, never." She replied. "I drive across town to the other Walmart. It's not safe here. This neighborhood has many illegal immigrants, and I would hear gun shots if I went shopping at that Walmart."

The fear shocked Allison. She wasn't sure how to take it. Could it really be that bad? She didn't feel unsafe. Sure, it was a different population, a different town, but it didn't feel bad to her.

Meanwhile, Mom's interview was comprised of many parts. Questions directed at Mom, simulations about ethical situations that arise in the doctor's office, group discussion about a mutually read article, and tours of the campus. The school was new, just graduating their first class the year prior, and yet they had big plans to grow. There would be another facility added on to the complex by the end of the year, and additional space constructed onto the main student building itself the following year. Class sizes were 75 currently and would become 125 by the next application cycle. The College of Osteopathic Medicine was the first of five health science programs to be opened in at the university.

"It felt comfortable." Mom commented after visiting. "I wouldn't want to be in the next class. I wouldn't want to be in a group any bigger with all the learning I would have to do. If they are going to let me in, I hope it is this year."

As the interview day finished, administrators informed students they would receive word of their admissions decision via phone call on February 2.

The second interview came and went, and admissions day grew closer. We distracted ourselves by talking about the waterfront that the Maine school neighbored, asking Allison to compare, again, the difference in the high schools she had visited. "What was it again the lady said she was scared of at Walmart?" We asked for the 50th time.

The day arrived. It was a week day, regular day of school and work in our house. Mom stayed next to the phone all day, waiting, hoping for a phone call.

"Mom! Did you hear from the school yet?" we each asked upon arrival home from school.

"Nothing yet." She replied, less and less enthusiastic each time.

5pm CST arrived and she hadn't heard anything.

"That's it, girls. I didn't get in."

"Really? How can that be?" We worked so hard to find her the perfect interview suit, could it really be gone? Her dream of becoming a doctor, the carrot, so close to her reach and yet still unachievable?

Ring-Ring. It was 5:05pm. Her phone had an incoming call from an unknown number.

"Hello?" Mom answered. "Yes, this is Karen. Yes. Yes. Ok. Thank you." She hung up the phone, and turned to us.

"I got in!"

We squealed in delight. "They accepted you?" we asked back,

hope lining our loud tones.

"I got in!" She repeated, "I got in. I got in. I got in."

A few days later, she had an email from the school in Maine, and wasn't accepted.

"I don't know if I should accept the position in WA." She expressed.

"Mom, you can't say no to this. You have to go. You've wanted this your whole life." I talked back.

"I just wish more than one place would say that I CAN do this. It is not comforting knowing only one place thinks I'm worth it to give this chance."

"Mom, you only need one ticket to go back to medical school, and this is it. One ticket. And you got it."

"But what about you girls? What about our life here? Can we really pick up and move halfway across the country?"

"We've done it before," I retorted.

"But that was for your Dad," she answered back. "The world was less scary with him beside me."

"Mom. We aren't letting you turn this down. You need to do this. We will figure the rest out later."

The next months passed in a blur. We had from February until July to change the course of our lives and prepare Mom for her next step. As my first year of college came to a close, I spent many weekends away from friends and campus to help pack. We had 10 years of our lives situated under one house, and now we had to pick up and move. The last time we moved for Dad's job I was eight years old.

We listed the house with a realtor, and began the enormous task of working through our belongings to remove clutter and make our house look bright, shiny, and appealing for interested parties. The closet we left untouched for years, a black hole of trinkets and junk had to be faced. Yes, what did take abode in that closet? Where does it belong now?

One Saturday, I tackled the American Girl Corner. At the bottom of the stairs in the basement was a corner nook that we added some cupboards and a large dollhouse shaped shelving unit, which housed our American Girl Dolls and their accumulated accessories. In theory, the stroller, high chair, bunk bed units were the only items that didn't fit nicely along the wall, and yet often the corner was only a moment or two from total explosion into the walkway with clothing, shoes, underwear, hair clips, and that random tie, which we never knew how to adorn on the dolls. This. This was a corner that needed some serious attention before anyone saw our house.

Even as we spent weeks sorting through clothes, the piles of papers on the bookshelf and in the kitchen, or the box of winter hats and mittens in the mudroom, there was always another corner. Had anyone looked next to the piano? Aha. A hidden junk compartment was there. What about inside the hexagon living room table? Gah! More papers, crayons, paper clips, and a piece of something that must have some use, but what could it be?

The showings began without much notice. One day we still had lots of toothpaste caked onto the sink in our bathroom, and the next day we were informed by our realtor there was a showing.

"Girls! I just got a call from the realtor. She said a family wants to see the house tomorrow at 9am!" Mom yelled, her voice ringing through the house as we all abided in our preferred hangouts. "We are going to need to clean bathrooms, vacuum, dust, and make sure as much clutter as we can is put away. They are going to take pictures of the house to put online at the same time."

Uffdah. The helping hands to make such deadlines possible were many, and our house once again became a place where busy bees could be found around every corner. This time, people weren't gathering to keep our house running as my family and I were trying to make car accident and dead Dad add up.

Instead, they were here to help our dreams, and most importantly Mom's dream, come true.

Given this move and return to school was for Mom, many people asked us how we felt about Mom going back to medical school. One day, Lily was laughing in the car because she had finally figured out the best response to give, "I'm excited…but a little bit bummed."

"Why Lily?" I asked.

"Because as much as people think it's cool and exciting to move, they are sad we are leaving. I have to leave my friends. I won't be able to quilt at church on Thursdays. I won't get to be a freshman at Mayo High School. The world my friends know is voluntarily no longer going to be mine. So, I just say 'I'm a little bit bummed' and that seems to satisfy them."

She was right. Anytime I had a chance to hear Lily respond to an inquiry for her opinion on the situation, "I'm excited…but a little bit bummed." She smirked, and then walked away.

Not everyone thought Mom going back to school and moving was a good idea. Or rather, the fear of uprooting a family, quitting her job, embarking on an education at high cost, and moving across the country, didn't seem to outweigh the benefits of returning to school.

"You have fucked up your life. And dragged your daughters into it too," doubt said.

"It was ruined the day Dave died in the accident and that has nothing to do with me. I know, it's crazy. I know. But I have to do this." Mom's gut responded.

"This time it's your fault. This time it's on you," fear added.

Self-doubt is powerful, and when voiced by those around us, the doubt and fears can take on force of their own. But, there is so much listening to do in the world. There is so much sound, noise, pain, joy, all the little voices. They speak and who listens? The signs, the heart, the destiny, the intuition, the collective voice of the world. Who listens? Mom did. There is so much listening to do in the world.

Later that day, my mom called me to tell me about this conversation.

"Kirsten, maybe I am being horribly irresponsible. Maybe I can't do this. Maybe this isn't what your dad would have wanted for you. Am I ruining your life?"

I was infuriated that anyone could claim our lives as "fucked up" yet. Medical school was only beginning. It was a long train to ride, and as challenging as it was to start, we hadn't even gotten there yet.

"Mom. No. Stop. Yes, you are afraid. Yes, we are afraid. We don't know what this means, how this will be for us, but don't you ever think for one minute that we are not going to make you try. We have not gotten this far for you to turn back before even getting there."

"But how can I provide for you, be your mother, when I'm studying all the time? How can we risk 4 years without any income?"

"I don't know, Mom. I don't know what will happen. It's worth it though. You being happy, you having a fresh start, you finding something, anything to believe in again is worth it. Worth the risk, worth the ambiguity, worth the unknown."

"I was talking to Dr. Fischer yesterday too about the mess I've gotten us into. He said the only way he has been able to come to terms with decisions, good or bad, in his past is to realize 'It seemed like a good idea at the time.'"

"That's good. That's helpful, right? 'It seemed like a good idea at the time.'"

As my mom's large professional discernment experience was underway, the house showings we had frantically prepared for in the spring weren't proving fruitful. Mom opted to continue as owner of our house, and instead put her efforts into finding renters to live in the place while she was at school.

With a new contract drafted and signed by all parties, we had until June 30, 2012 to move out of our house. Starting July 1, we slept at friends' homes across town for 11 days before we hopped in our car and made the road trip to Washington. We packed as much as we could, leaving our dogs behind temporarily at my aunt and uncle's and hit the road. Even though I was employed for the summer, my boss as he knew exactly our situation was flexible and gave me two weeks off to drive the Washington bound crew to their new home.

Did we know what to expect?

No way.

Did we have any idea what we were getting ourselves into?

Not at all.

Were we terrified?

Oh yeah.

Were we filled with hope?

Definitely.

White Coats

Mom began medical school five years after our car accident. The white coat ceremony which marked the beginning of the training took place on August 11, 2012. *Exactly* five years later.

It had taken effort from an entire village to get my family moved and physically settled into the new place. When Mom and Heidi got there, it was clear they were not in MN anymore. Yakima was desert. It was in the foothills. Our rental house was on a giant anthill. The backyard was full of goat head thorns. The windows looked out to Mount Adams on a clear day. Fortunately for Mom, Yakima has a ridiculously high number of days with sun each year. Sunlight wasn't going to be a problem.

"Why aren't there trees?" Heidi wanted to know. "I don't understand why there aren't trees."

A few weeks before the white coat ceremony inducting a new class of medical students, Mom called me and said, "Kirsten, I had a message on my phone from someone at the medical school. I was so worried they were going to tell me this was all a mistake. They didn't actually accept me into medical school."

"Mom! Why would you say that? They can't do that." I exclaimed.

"Or could they?" She countered. "I called them back already though, and it was a lady asking if I would be the student speaker for the white coat ceremony."

"What's that?"

"It's a little ceremony they do when we get the white coats that we will wear during medical school. It's supposed to be symbolic."

"Oh, ok."

"They asked me if I would be the student speaker. Guess what day it is?"

"I don't know." I responded. Mom and Heidi had been in Washington since mid July, and I honestly didn't have the timeline straight as to when different parts of the story came together. After moving Mom and Heidi to Washington, I came back to Rochester for a summer job. Lily and Allison were also spending their last few weeks with friends. Something like that.

"August 11." She said.

I paused. "What?"

"Did you know August 11 was going to fall on a Saturday again this year? I think it must be the first time since our car accident." She continued. "I know." She said responding to my stunned silent reaction.

"You have to do it." I responded. "You have to."

"What am I supposed to say? I don't know what I am getting myself into any more than these other whipper snappers here."

"That's not true. You saw Dad while he was in medical school. You have lived and watched the life a physician for so long. Tell them about Lily in the hospital, and all the reasons why you want to be a doctor, why her injuries pushed you over the edge because the physicians weren't treating the whole patient and that's how you found osteopathy and why you had to go for it."

"I suppose. I'm just not very good with words." She says. "You're the one that writes, would you help me?"

"Sure." I said. If living with my dad for 17 years didn't teach her how to tell a story, I didn't know what could. "Sure, I'll help. This is amazing. Congratulations, Mom."

Home

During the first few weeks of Mom's medical school career in Yakima, I barely heard from her. I was curious about how the school year was going, but I also enjoyed the space. I was a sophomore at St. Olaf College, and I had space to do, think, try, be without phone calls each week from Mom.

"Kirsten, have you figured out what you're going to major in?"

"Well, I'm thinking I might do Philosophy and linguistics."

"Why don't you take another biology class? That would really help you for working in a lab at Mayo Clinic this summer. I mean, you don't have anything else organized for summer yet, right? I just think 'Look at me', if you don't take the prerequisites for medical school now it's a lot harder to go back later."

The spring before she moved to Yakima, I heard this phone conversation like a broken record. Parents trying to encourage their children not the make the same mistakes they did. Mom trying to live out her dream of becoming a doctor through me.

When she started school, everything changed.

She had days full of orientation, site visits around town, and then classes, labs, and study groups through the waking and sleeping hours of the day.

It was mid October before I finally heard from her, "Hi

Mom! How are you? How are things going?" I asked eagerly.

"Kirsten, if I didn't love it so much, I think I would be crying the whole time. It's so hard, and there's so much work. I have so much to learn." She was doing it. She had found herself inside and was bringing that Karen to life again. I was exquisitely happy for her.

A few weeks later, for Thanksgiving I made my first trip to Yakima. I got off the tiny airplane which brought me over Mount Rainier National Park, and saw my sisters waving enthusiastically in a crowd outside of security. I ran to give them a hug, and Mom said, "Get her in the car. She's going to drive. Let's see how well she remembers her way around Yakima from that visit we took in March to look for houses."

"Challenge accepted." I said, climbing into the car.

I drove us through the airport parking lot, to the exit, and up to 74th avenue where I knew our house was. As I turned on the correct street, I could see the name as I turned, I heard someone in the back seat draw in a quick breath.

"Don't tell her anything," Mom joked. I drove up the hill and parked the car in our garage.

"Ha! Look at that. I made it." I exclaimed triumphantly.

"Yeah…" Allison answered from the back seat of the car. "Except that isn't a real road. We can't drive on it because it's a private street."

"What?!"

"We can't drive on that road because the owners don't want thru traffic. We have to go another way around." Mom explained, winking at me. "But you still got us here, I suppose."

Walking into a house I had never seen before, I was stunned by how familiar the place felt. With a fireplace, our red rug from City Grandma, the flowered couch Mom and Dad had upholstered, and the family portrait hanging in the main hall, it felt comfortable for an unfamiliar place.

"What do you think?" Mom asked. "Does it feel like home?"

I smiled. "Yes. Yes, it does."

"What is home?" Mom asked at dinner. "Is it the people you are with? The house you live in? The place we are? What does home mean for you, Kirsten?"

"I don't know, Mom." I whined, not sure how to answer or begin to understand the question.

"I think it's all of those things." Heidi chimed in.

"We need the people for sure, but the place, and the things help it also be more like a home." Allison stated.

"But are we at home in Yakima now?" asked Mom. "I feel more at home, more sure, and comfortable whenever I had my four daughters, my four pillars with me."

"We aren't always going to be together," I reminded her with a snarky chide.

"Lily, what do you think, where is home?" Mom asked, ignoring me.

"I'm just saying I think things are pretty homey right now." She responded with a smirk.

"But what about my house?" Mom continued. "This isn't my house. This house is built on an anthill, it has no insulation, the framing falls off the walls. I bought a house, a nice house, one that your Dad and I wanted in Rochester, and now I don't even get to live it. Some renters do, who charge me every month for damage that wasn't there before. We knew where our house was fragile, and we took care of it. I don't have my house."

"Maybe you feel the house is so important because you want to provide a space for us. We are your children and you feel you need to have the home for us to grow up in. We are growing up though, regardless, and you being in Yakima, in this house with or without insulation is important for us to do," Allison said.

"Speaking of which, I've got to go and study. We have three quizzes tomorrow and one is pharm. I can't remember all the names of these drugs. Chemistry was never my forte anyway. That was your dad's." She briskly walked away.

Lily leaned over to me, nudged, and whispered, "Did you notice the wall behind Mom? We made it into a white board, and it is pharm today, but yesterday it was GI.

"That," she said pointing to a drawing on the board, "Yep. It says fecal matter. Enjoy the rest of your dinner."

Styrofoam Filling

When the family structure is based on two parents, every single parent family out there is only half of what it can be. Less than half, when I think about how two parents adds up to more than just two adults but the foundation of the entire family. It's a situation of the whole being greater than the sum of its parts.

A single mom left without a husband after a sudden car accident loses more than the one adult that died behind the driver's wheel. We lost an entire half of the foundation of the family. Years of time from each of us daughters trying to make up the other half of the foundation manages to fill the void with lots of small pieces of Styrofoam. They take up the space, but sometimes there are gaps and sometimes it just makes a lot of noise when we put pressure on it as it readjusts to the weight of our family.

Fall of my senior year of college, I had just returned from nine months of studying abroad and working internationally at an ethnographic museum. I was a Spanish major, Student Director of the office I worked in at school, President of the Spanish house, and founder of an initiative to foster creative living. I had done so much. I had been away from the day to day of my family so long, I barely knew what it was like anymore. Heidi and Lily sent me homework questions they had. I remember one day looking through an essay Lily wrote thinking, "Since when did she become a junior in high school? That was me yesterday."

My sisters were becoming the age I was when Dad died, and I felt like they didn't know who I was. I didn't know who they were either.

"I did another round of interviews today for jobs," I told my mom over the phone.

"Where would you live if you got any of these jobs?" she asked.

"Well, they are in a couple different places: Washington D.C., San Francisco, Boston, Minneapolis."

"What if you came to live in Yakima next year? I'm not going to be around very much because of rotations. There's that great place downtown you could work and speak Spanish. You could help with the TEDx conferences or get a job at that coffee shop in the train station."

"I don't know, Mom." I could feel my hesitance rising. Could I go back into our family space without bringing back the darkness again? I was finally doing things that were normal, or so I thought.

After I hung up, I did what I had begun to do anytime I felt like I was making a big decision. I went to bed knowing the next day I would wake up and live as if I had made the decision to move to Yakima. I would see how it felt, how I wore the decision, and then I could take it off at the end of the day, sleep, and wake up the following morning and put on a new decision, maybe San Francisco, and see how that felt.

Beep Beep Beep Whack!

I slammed off my alarm the next morning.

"Today, I'm moving to Yakima," I told myself. I went to breakfast in the cafeteria. I made myself a bowl of oatmeal, peanut butter, and banana chips. I felt calm. I went to class, one and then another. I had dance rehearsal. I felt easeful. The floor really was my friend again. I went to dinner with friends. I studied in the library, productive and was home by 9:30pm.

"I'm moving to Yakima," I said to myself again.

The decision felt so good to wear I didn't even bother trying on a different one.

That's what I did. I graduated college and moved back home, if home is a place I had never lived, in a house that I had visited a handful of times, surrounded by sisters who I knew four years before.

I bought groceries, retrieved the mail, took out the garbage, walked the dogs, dropped my sisters off at school, made a meal plan, cooked dinner, cleaned the kitchen, and anything else I could spend my finite supply of stored energy on. I got a job at a local farm-to-fork bakery and at an education nonprofit working with Mexican immigrants. I went to protests and marches, I went to conferences and coffees, I played with my dogs, and watched the mountain disappear and the stars come out as the sun set.

I became acquainted with my sisters as peers instead of 7 and 9 year olds who I had to take care of. They missed the bus this morning to school, now how are they going to get there? They need to use the car after school, what about how I am going to get to work? Problem solving became our forte. We got good at being resourceful, efficient, and celebrated each other when we made it through another day.

Single parenting for the first few years after the accident meant the family structure learned to balance on one leg with an occasional moment of shifting weight onto the mixed Styrofoam structure fashioned by us children to about the shape and size of the void of the other parent as best we could.

But the main part of that Styrofoam structure is that it was a team effort. Mom and every single on us of daughters has contributed, and we continue to contribute with our attitudes. Mom didn't let me give up, we don't let her give up. Lily learned how to make meal plans better than I did. We love it when she's in the kitchen. Heidi takes the dogs for runs each morning all by herself. She's big enough for that. I don't need to take care of her, or any of them. The more we supported each other the stronger we became as individuals, together. I was young, struggling, looking for any reason to force myself to keep moving. I projected a responsibility onto myself that wasn't true, and never probably was from the beginning.

"Remember those times when you ran off to go to the bathroom instead of doing the dishes?" Allison asked me. "That was when Dad called me to help him. You've never done it alone. We've always been building this life together. You don't need to take care of us. What do you need to take care of you?"

Forgetting can be beautiful

Sometimes I forget. I forget that I am broken, I forget that I am hurting. Those are strange and beautiful moments. They happen more often the more I come into myself. My mom made the analogy once that the hurt stays the same size my entire life. The hurt stays the same, but I grow. I get older, I keep living, and through living I have more experiences and create an identity that is no longer only encompassed in the black hole of loss, but it's also something else beyond that. It's like the entire timeline of my life was on white paper and dark ink spilled and splashed over the entire page.

But life keeps going. Sometimes I wish I could freeze time, but I can't. With each passing minute or second there is just a little bit more of the paper that is new, white, and without the stain on it. The hurt stays the same size, but its proportion to my identity shrinks. That's a horrible and beautiful sensation all at the same time.

How could my Dad ever mean less to me? Maybe I am not just the black letters "death" scarred across my forehead. Maybe I have a worth beyond that, and maybe just maybe my life is still filled with possibility.

Transmission

On the car ride home from church one Sunday in Yakima, Heidi said, "I just feel so bad about myself all the time. I feel guilty for wasting time. I feel guilty about doing something I want to do. I feel like I'm becoming the person I don't want to be."

The calm I felt the first few months I lived there, and the groove we'd found for this new family passed quickly into great uncertainty. The final year of medical school meant interviews. Mom had 14 interviews around the country in 3 months in order to rank her top choices for where she wanted to go after graduating for her Family Medicine Residency.

"Womb to tomb. That's my kind of medicine," She said. After interviewing and ranking, all we could do was wait. The computer system matched the residency program preferences with student preferences and once Mom was "matched" that was her place for the next three years. Heidi would move with Mom, Allison and Lily would both be in college, and me? I had no idea what I would do next.

"Why? How so?" I asked Heidi. Realizing throwing back "Why?" was probably not the best way to approach the conversation, I tried again.

"I mean, can you be more specific? Can you tell me examples or characteristics of what you notice you don't want to be?"

"I feel like I'm angry at my friends all the time. I can't stand to be around them. I feel like a classic teenager."

"Can you tell me more what that means? What that looks like? And how that's different from who you want to be?"

"My friends always make me feel like everything is a competition. And yet, at school, I wish people would be nicer. I was nice to the foreign exchange students once and now they are always with me because no one else welcomes them. I feel better hanging out with the guys than the girls because they are chill and there is less pressure and competition. The competition makes me feel anxious all the time."

"That sounds like this is a matter of identifying who Heidi is, distinct from the environment she finds herself in."

"And, it's stressful. I don't know where I'm going to be next year. I'm afraid of being alone. You'll be gone, Allison will be away studying abroad, Lily will go to college, and Mom will be working all the time wherever she goes to residency. I will be all alone."

"It's hard, isn't it? Not knowing the future?"

"Yes. My friends' parents make me so frustrated too. Like one parent is always at every cross country meet, she controls what her daughter eats and knows every homework assignment and when it is due."

"Do you want me to come to every meet for you?"

"No, I don't want that. I don't want you to sacrifice who you are for me. That makes me feel more guilty. I guess I feel deprived of having parents."

"Well, that's true. You are right. We don't have parents in the same way that your friends do."

"And their parents do so much for them. To me, it seems like their lives are so easy. And I try to do the same things, but I have to work for it. It's so hard, and makes me angry. They don't understand how hard I work to try to do the same things," Heidi continued.

"Isn't that frustrating?" I asked, "Especially, when people say, 'Oh, your dad died because God knew you could handle it.' Like hell. You are telling me I was forced into this sucking life because I could handle it? That's not fair. That's a cruel world."

"Right. And my friends don't understand. They think they do but they don't. Mom's doing a great job, it's not that, it's just I want Dad back."

The conversation paused.

"I know. And, no matter how hard Mom tries she is only one person, she can't make up the difference between having two parents and only having one," I said.

"I am so scared about forgetting, Kirsten. I don't feel like I remember who Dad is."

The conversation paused again. We were pulling into the driveway of the rental house now.

"Here, let's go watch some videos. You can see them, hear his voice, and remember."

"Yeah, but I don't like doing that. Because then, my memories of Dad are made up, they are memories of the videos, not actual memories of him."

Sigh.

"Yes. I'm sorry," I said to her.

"I don't want to forget him, Kirsten."

It's disempowering. It's a sock in the gut. It's the most helpless and debilitating feeling to not want to forget, and yet to recognize I can never remember. Memories fade. That's what happens. And, no matter how hard we try, time and space come into our lives and the vivid experience of one time becomes, "Oh, yeah, I think I remember that" and eventually, "When did that happen?"

I took Heidi to watch some videos that Dad made. When we were young, he pulled out the video camera at the slightest whim and began recording what was going on in our lives. From a sassy Lily who completely ignored him in one video, a baby Heidi learning to crawl in the living room, Allison sitting in our mini blue chair watching a movie, to Kirsten in the kitchen with Mom making sugar cookies, we have a few day to day moments captured on tape. Dad, as the filmmaker, rarely makes an appearance in the films, but he narrates. He probes at the enfolding scene, teasing Allison to give him a smile, or asking

Heidi to say "Hello, Mom!" in the picture. It's all we need though. Hearing his voice is hearing how much he cared about us, how totally devoted he could be to supporting the world of his young daughters.

But, after 1 minute and 22 seconds, the tapes end. We can play it again, but Dad will say the same thing. Another and another time and it's just one scene of our lives repeated on end. It's not today. It's not Dad. It's just a recording, and walking away from the screen means reality washing back down over us. We can't bring him back. He will never produce new sounds, phrases, or sentences for us to hear. He is silenced forever.

The next week, I am waiting in the car after church again. We are trying to leave church for groceries. Heidi is in the process of getting her driver's license, and when we have a few extra minutes in our commute or we really don't care about being late, she gets to drive.

"It's all about practice." Mom tells her, and it's true.

The more practice, the better she gets at driving. After she is done though, Mom takes the wheel again.

"Goodness, that girl has short legs." Mom complained as she sat down. "It's just like her father. He was taller than me, but I always had to move the seat back when I got in the car after he was driving. He had short legs and so does she. He got a good dose of his genes in that child. That, and her personality too. Just like him."

Only a day before I was sitting on the couch with my knees up to my chest and my arms wrapped around my knees. My eyes were red from crying, and Heidi walked in the door.

"Is something wrong?" She immediately asked.

"No." I said, putting on a smile for her. It's good to see her after the day. "Just lots of ups and downs and emotions. That's what writing and memories do to me. Come here."

She sat down behind me and I leaned onto her shoulder and started to cry again.

"It's ok." She cooed, petting my hair.

"It's just so sad sometimes," I said. "I meet people and want people to be in my life so we can actually live together, not just so that I can learn from them. Just because I've learned a lot from Dad, I don't want him to be gone. But he is anyway. He was just someone I learned some good things from and now I have to live on without him."

"At least you knew Dad." She said. "I feel like the only thing I know of him is an idea, a memory, that's not even mine. I don't know who he is or what he was like."

She doesn't see it in herself, but nature and nurture are strong. We think we are our own people. Yet Lily, Heidi, and I laugh how often Allison and Mom fight about something because they both are exactly the same: stubborn and totally convinced the other person will give in first, to the point of speaking words they wish they both could take back. But they can't pull the vibrations of the vocal chords back into their throats after the words have been yelled.

Sometimes, Allison, Lily, Heidi and I can't tell how much like Mom or Dad we are. Yet, waiting in the car that Sunday morning with Mom, Lily runs into the car almost immediately after I texted her we were waiting for her and Heidi.

"Where is your sister?" Mom inquired.

"Heidi is talking to Pastor Nowak. She had to find some more creamer before we left."

"Talking." Mom chuckled to herself. "Just like her father." The apple doesn't fall far from the tree.

I want to share the memories I have of Dad, but I suppose I can't really transmit them to Heidi. Isn't it interesting how something can be rooted in an experience of reality that I have and archived in my mind as a memory? Then, I can share that memory with someone else, except for them it is only an idea. It starts in their head, and will stay in their head, unless they decide to try and recreate it, much like Heidi may try to recreate an experience of Dad. As soon as they have taken my memory now transformed into their idea and make it into a recreated reality and experience, it becomes a new memory. It's a new memory all over again. What then continues to be transferred? The essence? The emotional quality? The cute story which creates a particular emotional tone? The sound that was so enjoyable and pleasing it was worth creating again?

Creating and recreating are in fact the same thing. *"A"* causes there to be an inspiration for creating *"B"*, and recreating comes from being re-inspired to create *"B"* again.

Buddha said if you are truly present and enjoying life there is no need to ever experience the same thing again. Even when we are children, though we desire repetition. "Daddy, let's go down the slide again!" "I want another candy…pleeease?" Isn't that related to the concept of practice, why we value patterns and rhythm. Are we setting ourselves into a paradox? We preach precision of enjoyment for a specific moment, and yet the practice of accomplishment demands repetition?

Sometimes I also worry that he doesn't know me, just like Heidi worries she doesn't know him. Since the moment he died, I've changed, we've changed. Does Dad even know? Has he even seen the best nuggets of what have come out of the worst thing that ever happened to me?

"Yes, he does," a voice inside me says. "He knows."

That is a relief.

It's a relief because it means we are still a family. Just like I am working on how to be a big sister to grown up little sisters, I can acknowledge that Dad would have to change to be a Dad of four grown daughters. We can look back in the tapes and remind ourselves of how he used to talk or how his face looked when he was most at ease, but in the end, we are different people now, it's a different time, and that's just one moment from a distant past. No matter how well we can transmit the memories forward, they change as we change, and that's how recreating makes us new again.

Eyes

I visited a friend who studied abroad with me about a year and a half after we had last seen each other. She became my friend because she genuinely wanted to practice Spanish, and many other students were interested in other diversions. She looked at me from across the couch where we were sitting, chatting about all that we had done since we last saw each other; the new worries and decisions sitting on our shoulders. She said, "You have age in your eyes. People our age don't have that, but you do. You've had responsibility and experienced things most of us can't even imagine. And it's aged you. We can see it in your eyes."

Recurrence

While I lived in Yakima, my now alma mater asked me to participate in a workshop in Seattle. I spent four days with university students eager to discern their career path as if it were as easy as answering a question correctly or incorrectly on a standardized test. Several staff members accompanied the group, facilitating the conversation with us, the alumni.

During one day, we traversed the waterfront in downtown Seattle, and eventually climbed on a ferry to Bainbridge Island. It was a cool day, the mist spritzed my face and a heavy wind pushed me inside from the deck. I found myself in conversation with one of the staff members I had been meaning to catch up with.

"So, tell me more about what you are doing now," He prodded.

"I'm living in Yakima, where my family moved three years ago. I moved after graduation in May and I started work in the bakery at an orchard. In August, I started working at the nonprofit where I am now."

"Are you living at home?" He clarified. I felt failure wash over me.

"Yes." I answered, my face heating.

"And how old are your sisters?"

"I have three. One is in college now. Two are still in high school, and Mom is finishing her last year of medical school." I answered, trying to justify why I would have moved back home after graduating from a proud liberal arts college rather than out into the world somewhere.

"Where's your dad?" He asked, "I remember parts of your story, but not all the details."

I take less than a moment to pause. If I pause too long, he'll know something isn't normal. Yet, I need to brace myself in order to nonchalantly spit out the words that I so desperately wish were not true.

"He died in a car accident in 2007."

"Were you in the car?" He asked.

Pause. *Don't feel it. Don't feel the pain. Just answer the question.*

"Yes. We all were. That's a big part of the reason I moved in with my family this year. It's been a long time since I've reconnected with them, and we have changed and grown since this happened. My mom needs the support, it's her turn to feel something good for herself, and they supported me unconditionally while I did whatever I wanted at St. Olaf, so it's my turn. I enjoy repositioning my relationship with my younger sisters too, because they have become their own independent people since I last knew them well, and I want to continue to be relevant in their lives, which means I am more a peer than a manager." I spewed hastily trying to move the subject back to less volatile territory such as how proud I am of my mom and sisters.

"That's a very important task." He affirmed. "The relationship between siblings is a challenging one to renegotiate later in life, and with your experience I can imagine it is important to do so."

"Yes."

"Have you ever gone to a therapist? I mean a good therapist?" He asked.

What? I didn't think I had unwittingly shown how much I felt the darkness inside me. I thought I was rather composed.

"I did for a while in 2007. I stopped eventually because every time I went I had so much to fill her in on that I didn't feel as though I was walking away with any concrete progress. My mom mentioned to me one day that the appointments were expensive, and it dawned on me that I was spending the little money we had on something that wasn't particularly effective. I stopped, and haven't gone since. I preferred talking to friends."

"That makes sense. I've seen a therapist twice in my life, and my wife has seen several therapists, some better than others. Sometimes it is helpful to talk to someone who isn't mixing the conversation in with the larger context of how they relate to you and how what you express affects your relationship."

"Hm." I could see how that might be worthwhile. "How did you find a good therapist?" I asked.

"Mostly through our friends. Asking around, and seeing who different people recommended."

"Hm."

"It's been helpful for us, especially because my wife lost her father when she was 12 years old. Different times in our marriage have called back deep grief that neither of us expected. When we wanted to have children, for example, she became very sad and went to therapy for a long time, coming to terms with how to enter a parent-child relationship on her own when she lost her parent at a young age."

I didn't know this about him. I wanted to ask, "What is it like to be with someone who is forever grieving a loss from before you knew them?" I held myself back.

"That makes a lot of sense." I responded. "I have noticed in myself periods of increased grief for any number of reasons, sometimes unidentifiable, and in time I've turned to writing more than anything else to help sort out what's in my head."

Our conversation was interrupted for a group photo in front of a mural, and the moment to ask how my future with grief might look was gone.

Lessons

A few months later, I received a message from a friend saying she was rushing out of town to join family at the bedside of a sister who had severe brain hemorrhaging and was in a coma. With every instance of suffering, every possibility of loss, every family tragedy I encounter I think I must have a better way to approach this situation than the last one. I must have learned something, and be better able to navigate of these challenging situations, right?

Reading news from my friend in her text, I had nothing to say. I couldn't make a comment about the situation without knowing details, and even then it's hard to think what would be comforting instead of hurtful. I do not have the answers. I do not have words to express the situations and feelings I have found myself in, but even so I do know *something*.

Once, my mom and Allison were arguing about priorities and trying to decide logistics about a travel situation, involving many moving parts. My mom walked away from the conversation defeated, stressed, and desolate. She closed herself in her room.

After a few minutes, I knocked on the door, not wanting her to be alone and feel as though her children were attacking her. She looked up at me with tears in her eyes and asked, "Can you please leave me alone?"

I felt my face flush. How did we do this to her? I left and thought for a while how to handle this situation. After an hour of distracting myself, I walked back over to her door and asked, "Mom, we are going to take the dogs for a walk, would you like to come with?"

"Yes," was the resounding response I heard through the door.

Within minutes, she emerged, bundled in scarf and fleece sweatshirt to bear the wind. We didn't say anything to each other as we walked. A time which for us is normally an opportunity to talk through ideas and concerns in our heads was instead entirely introspective. I was reminded in this moment how important supporting an individual who has experienced sadness, suffering, tragedy, loss in maintaining the rhythm of life that they value is the littlest thing, but also the best thing anyone can do. The silent routine spoke loudly. We were there for each other. We cared about the other person. We weren't going to give up from this one conflict.

As the days after our car accident turned into months, the small offerings of support, although often met with my frustration and desperation, were the critical steps in the direction of recovering a sense of movement again in my life. My dad's death stopped my world. The morning of August 11, 2007 might as well have halted the earth's rotation for all I felt. There was no time. There was no movement. There was no life as I knew it. Yes, I wanted to wallow in that place for a long time, because I thought I needed it to process what had happened. However, I never would have recovered my own momentum without the late night phone calls offering math tutoring one evening a week, or the rides to and from piano lessons, or the fall leaves which magically disappeared from the front lawn. Those small moments helped the engine of my life to ignite again.

And then, sure enough, one week of piano lessons leads to a month. One month of math tests accumulates to a year, and eventually time passed whether I realized it or not. I have learned to live again. That's what I have learned. I can offer something.

I can be with people I care about in silence. I can help find solid ground to walk on even when everything feels shattered or turned around. I have learned something. That's how I keep living with people I care about and the things that hurt.

Breath

Sometimes I need breath, sometimes I need it to blow out, to breathe out the things inside me, the toxic, contagious joy that comes from a spouting hole that found home inside me. And sometimes the breath is for my body. Not me. It keeps me pinned here. Because I'm here now. Even though he isn't. Dad isn't here now so he doesn't need breath. But he can be breath if he wants to be.

4-3-2-1

I promise, death is normal. It's not a crazy phenomenon that we look disappointedly at the people who happen to encounter it. Death is normal and death is everywhere. Just because I might be the oldest person in a group, doesn't mean I will be the first one to die.

Seeing my family as broken, seeing myself as broken because we've been touched by death, now I realize is hurtful and helpful.

It's hurtful because it reinforces a wrongness to our lives now; an incompleteness, lack of utility, accomplishment, meaning. Like the broken kitchen chair that sits in the garage because three of the four legs have fallen off, something broken is discarded, cannot be used or do anything anymore, and now what gave the chair meaning has been taken away.

This interpretation of my family is so very wrong. Since we "broke," we have graduated 3 daughters from high school and 2 from college with the highest marks, and Mom from Osteopathic Medical school. Heidi was one of the most popular student writers for the local newspaper, Lily was voted Prom Queen, and Allison received the most prestigious scholarship for upperclassmen at her university. Mom was asked to share her story on Story Corps with National Public Radio, a local writer asked to interview her, and her classmates elected her to speak at graduation. We moved from one state to another and will move again, made new friends, seen places unseen, we have grown closer and we are working to find the exact manifestation of our individual meaning in the way we live our lives today. Time doesn't stop, and the grieving continues. On the eve of accepting admission to a Ph.D. program, I felt sick in my gut because I wished so much that I could talk to Dad about what it was like for him to decide to get a Ph.D. But alas, here we are: 4 girls, 3 high schools, 2 states, 1 mom.

What's more, something that is broken associates negative emotions, like sadness, frustration, anger, yet people gravitate around our family in swarms. On a brief visit to Rochester, each sister notified one friend we were in town and within an hour, we were over 30 people standing in the front lawn of our old house talking, laughing, and enjoying each other's presence. People want to be with us. They want to help us, and we've been told it's because people enjoy our joy, gratitude and appreciation. That doesn't sound like a family that is not accomplished, or useful, or does not have meaning in their lives. I have to believe that means something about how we've grown from grief.

On the other hand, being a "broken" family does remind us of what makes us different from other people, what perhaps has pushed us in the direction of the use, meaning, and accomplishment we have today. If Dad hadn't died when I was 14, I may have spent years thinking he was annoying, rather than reminding myself of his memory and the goodness he put into the world by following his inspirations. The custodians at my school are my friends because I know he spent many late nights in the lab chatting with Kermit the custodian on the 5th floor where his research lab was during his Ph.D. at Mayo Clinic. He taught me they are people too, with families and lives outside of the work they do and that is fertile ground for a meaningful relationship with them.

Values like this have been slowly infused into the way I live now because of what happened to me. I used to spend hours wondering if I had been heading down a path with my life so

162

wrong and bad that I needed something to happen to me in order to get back moving in the direction that is meant for my life. I don't believe in a higher power that micromanages what happens when; I think coincidence and chance are causal forces in the world. Even so, I have to believe there is something that I am here for that is unique to me, my skills or goals, that is a sense of the true North that I can work to orient myself towards. Thus, I used to wonder if my brokenness was the realigning of my four wheels to move me in the northern direction. I was looking for a reason, a *porque*, for what happened to me. Now, I don't think like that because most days I can wake up and understand the randomness of what happened. The serendipity of it all. Even so, mention of the fact that I am broken reminds me of the accident that has driven me to be and do what I do now, and that is unique to who I am.

But I realize now I don't have to call myself "broken" to remember that intentionality for my life. I can look at a family picture of a happy moment from last year and see what's missing. That is enough to remind me.

In Kathryn Schulz's TED Talk about wrongology, she says "The miracle of your mind is you can see the world as it isn't. You can imagine the future; you can remember the past."

I can see in pictures of my mom, sisters, and I at the top of Bear Creek Mountain what isn't in our world today. That is enough. My past is not pieces of a ceramic pot crumbling in my hands, it's a story that I get to tell.

Anniversaries are days to remember. Generally, we associate them with happy moments, but I also have a sad anniversary every August 11. As we congratulate and celebrate on happy anniversaries, it would make sense that we experience sadness and receive consolation on sad anniversaries. But in 2015, I wasn't sad.

"Why aren't I sad today? It's August 11, 2015. It's my sad day, and I'm not sad." I tried taking my journal forcing myself to sit in a safe place, alone in the corner, and walked through moment by moment the sad things that happened on August 11, 2007.

But as much as I remembered sad things, I couldn't make myself sad. That's the point. As much as I couldn't make myself sad on my sad anniversary, I can't make myself happy on days that aren't the sad anniversary. I can't control the existence of emotions, nor am I always broken every August 11.

I can control how I respond to them. I can control how I let them affect me in a given moment, but I cannot create or destroy emotions.

Control can be sobering, it can be comforting, it can be calming because we know we can control things. But not being able to control my emotions is the first of a long list of items I cannot control in my life. In fact, not controlling my emotions demonstrates there is even little of me, my physical or emotional being that I can control. It's my mind. My attitude, my perspective and responses that I get to control. That's the rook I have to play in a game of chess where I have only one piece. It's terrifying, and it's freeing. Can you see how free I am?

We went hiking to Summerland and Panhandle Gap in the Mount Rainier National Park. As we began the slow incline up to the mountain valley, our hiking guru stopped us and said we all needed to pause and think about our heel toe. With the trekking poles and a good heel-toe, there is a little rest in each step while climbing. As we ascended up and up, I mediated on the heel-toe.

Heel-toe.

Heel-toe.

"Find the rest in each step," he said.

Sure enough, I could have climbed for days. I climbed and climbed and didn't feel the paralyzing burn in my quadriceps or gluteal muscles like I feel every time I mount the hill that leads to our house.

The rest in each step.

I couldn't help but notice the metaphor.

Certainly, my years of high school and college had been busy ones, and intentionally so. I chose to be busy at school, dedicate myself to my work while cursing it at the same time. I chose my commitments at college, and then added some more because I could. I ran around like crazy, putting on one face for one thing, another for another according to the context and what I deemed was appropriate. Sure, I'll host employers at the college. Sure, I'll speak with donors and prospective students. Sure, I'll share my ideas inside the classroom when no one else wants to speak. Sure, I'll dance all evening at practice. In high school, I used to need time to prepare for each new face every day, but by the time I was deep into the rigor of college, there was no time. It was a good thing I found improvisation and intuition at that time otherwise I would have never made it. As I prepared to leave for my time in Yakima I thought, after eight years, I could use a year of rest.

But from the moment my "year of rest" began, I was busy. I worked every week, volunteered, interviewed and prepared for a second job, wrote job applications, traveled to visit friends, embarked into the outdoors. I certainly slept, but rest wasn't the only occupation during this time.

The rest in each step.

That's a totally different approach to the way I live.

Find the rest in each step. Whether each step is a second, minute, hour, day, week, month, there is a rest in each step. And doing so I can climb higher and longer.

That also means letting the things inside myself come out. That means taking time to breathe where I didn't before. I want us to be able to find the rest, the release of those emotions and thoughts churning around inside of us in every step. Because, that's how we are going to keep going through the pain that weighs on our lives.

What does it mean that we don't know when the end is? What significance does that bring to our lives?

The end is the part of the cycle of life, whether we know when it is or not. My present is the only moment I can control, and even then sometimes I am the recipient of an effect caused by someone else's present.

How is it that end gives and takes meaning? Even using a person as a means or an end has a significant difference in what's ethical. Ends matter, they influence us. That's important to recognize.

And now, since I don't know my end, and you don't know yours, we get to live with the freedom of not knowing, and let's hope that we can live enough in the present to appreciate the moments that all add up to the same sum, end.

Skin

There was never a person more comfortable in his own skin. That's what people said about my dad after he was gone. He was overweight, he was smart, but he never felt less of a person for his large stature nor did he intend to build himself up by using his superior intellect and education to distance himself from people. He was comfortable in his skin, and people loved him for that. He must have enjoyed wearing it every day because it was comfortable. How lucky to have a skin that is nice to wear.

Mom matched to a residency program on the West side of the Cascade mountains. We had to sell the house in Rochester, Minnesota now. It was real; there was no going back. As we packed our boxes again to leave Yakima, I found a picture of Dad holding Allison and I on his lap in the pink chair. We are all looking directly at the camera. The picture is yet another lens, but maybe because this one caught our eyes, we can see into the souls of ourselves from another time.

As we age, our eyes are always the same, and yet when I see myself in different photos or look in the mirror from one day to the next, my eyes are different. They speak and show different trials and excitements of my soul. In the picture, my head is tilted, and that doesn't surprise me. I found as I searched through pictures that the times when I express utter joy in a moment, I tilt my head to the right. Every time.

In this picture, I am sitting on my dad's lap, he is holding my hand, and my head is tilted. I am joyful.

Allison has squinty eyes and her nose wrinkles the bigger she smiles. I am sure, I just know, if I looked through her pictures the wrinkles would appear in her happiest moments too.

'If I look at just our eyes, look at just the window of the soul: what do I see?' I wondered to myself.

I started with me, because it was easy. I see trust. I thought to myself. I see curiosity, I see the recognition of fear and unknown, but I see comfort and protection, and acceptance in that moment.

In Allison's eyes, I see challenge, I see adventure, I see spirit, she is feisty, assertive, confident, and innocent.

What do I see in Dad's eyes?

I see joy. I also see a big world and a small boy. I see an eagle soaring, in respect and in relish of what the world has to offer. I see one step at a time, I see luxuriating in moments, I see gathering up that which is important to him, that which he wanted to share with the world. I see a child as an adult, an adult as a father, a student as teacher. I see acceptance of hurt and embracing of gain. I see power and recognition of limited control. I see love, and I see a man living out his time as best he can with trust in himself, his love, and his world. I see a man comfortable in his own skin.

Dear Uncle Doug,

It was so wonderful to get your most recent letter! I'm relieved you still want to be pen pals when I was so slow to respond!

Yes, speaking of rain and storms, it's been really quite stormy this last week. I can see lots of down branches and much in disarray when I walk to campus after the storming. The power has gone out several times too. It's snowing today only two hours east of where I am. They claim it's the last snow of the season; we'll see.

Early spring in Minnesota always makes me skeptical. I never know until July whether winter is really at bay!

I was at a workshop a few weeks ago for my Ph.D. program, and we had to introduce ourselves and describe how we were doing with weather language. I said, "This is probably only meaningful to Minnesotans but I feel like a bright, sunny day when it's negative 30 degrees outside. Biting, beautiful, and a reminder we're still very alive." That got some cheers from the two other Minnesotans in the room.

Lily is recovering well from her trip to the hospital. Hard to believe this was the first time in 10 years she's had any problems from the accident. It brought us all back to those weeks in the hospital with a 9-year-old girl who just wanted to go home. She came to visit me last week and claimed she was back to swinging normally. Apparently, she was also able to get caught up on all the schoolwork she missed. That was almost equally as impressive of a recovery. I can't imagine how resilient she is. She also just found out she got a job as a Resident Assistant on campus next year, so she is very excited.

Heidi also came to visit me with Lily. She has been so busy taking standardized tests for college applications. She's in her junior year of high school, and time is flying so quickly. I hope she does as well as she's been trying with all the effort she's used studying. I certainly didn't do as much preparation as she has.

Allison found out this week that she got a job too! She will be working as a middle school math teacher. She said it was the hardest interview she's done yet, but they offered her the job right on the spot when she finished. Seems like a good sign.

I met some former colleagues of my dad recently who now are working at Stanford. It was such a heartwarming and heartbreaking experience simultaneously. I learned more about who he was for the people that saw him when he was away from us kids and that's a unique window. Very special to hear about.

I went skiing a few weeks ago, I think the same day you wrote your most recent letter, and it was very refreshing to be outside the concrete jungle in the city. The semester will finish the last week of April, so that's keeping me on my toes.

Mom is staying very busy too. She's been delivering babies as an OB/GYN this month. She loves the womb to tomb aspect of family medicine.

I'm so glad to hear Lisa is doing better. Wow! How impressive what a difference a procedure like that can do. Sounds like both her and Jack keep the place busy! How fun you made some trips to Phoenix. It must mean so much to Ethan that you come out for his games, and it's awesome he's had such a good season.

I'll ask Heidi if there's videos we can send you of the band. They just had a concert last weekend too, so I'm sure there's something recorded. Say hello to Lisa and Jack for me. I hope March ended like a lamb and April showers aren't too heavy!

Love, Kirsten

The Family Circle

I will never stop wondering. I will always ask questions. Everything I see, do, notice, experience is an opportunity to wonder: why did this happen to me? How am I supposed to keep going? Now, if I'm lucky I can silent those voices in my head for a few moments and let my attention drift, follow my curiosity, the buzz of the passing bumblebee.

In the demographic sense, life is the absence of death. A professor exclaimed during one lecture, "Congratulations! You've succeeded in not dying. You've lived!"

As counter-factual as it may seem, it is valid. Maybe it feels simplistic or maybe it feels unrealistic, but the point is life-as-not-dying is freedom.

Congratulations!

The pressure is off.

I did it! I lived!

Now, what am I going to do with my freedom?

It's like the concept of grace within the Lutheran church. No longer do I need to spend my life enslaved to this existential question of what is my life, what is my purpose, instead I have grace. I am saved and I don't need to do anything to get grace. I have been wiped clean, set free, and now I can do anything. Anything. That's amazing.

Even though we are within this larger operation, we have a sense of agency. We get to choose how we spend our freedom. Who we are, what we become, how we respond to the mechanism in which we live are the ways in which we control our lives. Sure, we experience things we never planned. We are hurt by the death of someone we love. We hurt when someone leaves us behind, but we hurt because the camaraderie, the connection with other people, beyond ourselves, is enriching. It gives us something outside of our own that we cannot control but still resonates within us. That kind of synchronicity is a worthy endeavor with our freedom. Being ourselves with another person, the people we care about and who care for us, is

Indescribable. . .

Even now, I'm still figuring out how to be in my skin, in society, with people and my pain. When I moved to start college, I was excited to have a clean slate. I was ready not to be the broken, hurt child, so I didn't tell people my story. If someone talked about his/her dad, I would talk about mine. If someone asked what my dad did, I would say: "He was a geneticist." Most people never noticed the past tense.

Eventually with friends, I get to the point where I can't be me without them knowing my story. It shapes what I do, it shapes how I think, it shapes how I feel, it shapes what I believe. It shapes who I am and they need to know my story to know me. Sometimes I bring it up, just like when I brought up to my friends in fourth grade that I wasn't normal. I had a hole in my heart, a Ventricular Septum Defect that eventually closed on its own. Life threatening or not, I thought it important my friends know, so I said to them all once at a sleepover.

"Everyone stop. I have something I need to tell you. I have a hole in my heart." "So what?" My friends responded, and we kept playing.

On one hand this seems like a phenomenal response. My

fourth grade friends didn't care about that, they were my friends no matter what. But then again, I know now I would have appreciated them asking me about this hole in my heart.

"Is it big?"

"Does it hurt?"

When the hole in my heart was no longer physical, but rather emotional, this situation played out almost identically. I would tell someone my story, usually when I could no longer answer questions without lying, and they would pause, "Oh," look away, and start talking about something else.

Every so often there was the person that although shocked, asked me about it. We may have talked for several hours after I first told them, indication enough for me they respected who I was. My true friends continue to ask me about my story. They never stopped caring about my hurt, and they never expected me to stop wanting to talk about it. They knew me enough to know I want to talk about it.

Sometimes trying to share my story with people just didn't work. Either I said too much too quickly, or I said something too sad too blasé. Or, once I told my story and the person cried. For a long time, this response made me angry. I thought, 'I have barely gotten to a point where I can tell my story without crying and this softie across the table from me threatened that calm when he began bawling!'

I found myself comforting him saying "It's ok. Don't cry. I didn't mean for you to cry."

I thought, 'I am the one hurt; I should be the one to cry, and now I am supposed to be gracious and let someone else cry over MY PAIN? Let me tell you, it was a hell of a lot more sad, more hurtful, and more difficult LIVING through it than listening to it.'

I was angry.

Now, I realize it's not my fault or anyone's how this interaction goes. There isn't a universal guidebook for how to ask everyone about tough subjects or how to respond to hearing something tragic come up while I'm taking my last sip of mocha.

The point is that it's practice. Practice picking myself up again and trying. Trying to meet someone new. Trying to share myself. Trying to find connection again. Trying. Sometimes it won't work, but that's all the more reason to try. Whether it's people, friends, or new things, I know now that I'm going to spend my freedom turning over every stone if I have to. For as long as I keep breathing, that effort is worth it.

When I was little, at night I would imagine what would happen if someone broke into our house. When I played with my American Girl dolls the next day I would reenact the plans, each doll representing a sister and me as the parent. When the situation of danger approached, I gathered all my dolls into our home, walls built from couch pillows and blankets as roofs. We would huddle together, my voice calming them:

"It's ok, Kirsten. Don't be afraid. Erin, stick close and it will be just fine."

And then the moment of truth would happen. The danger would be close enough that someone needed to do something, and clearly it was going to be the strongest, bravest of us all; that was me. I went to fight off the danger, throwing pillows and kicking wildly, until I was victorious, had saved my doll family, and returned back inside the house of pillows to calm the frantic nerves of my dolls.

In our real family, I had lined us up in my head according to strength, braveness, and age. Naturally, Dad was our first line of defense. He would take out the bad guy while Mom held us all safely in the hiding spot. If reinforcements were needed, Mom would go help Dad, because we didn't want him to get stretched too thin as to lose the fight, and I would take over as defender of my sisters and our hiding place. If someone were sneaky enough to get around both my parents, it was up to me to protect anything that was left, and so on down the line of sisters.

This emergency line-up I had envisioned in my head didn't turn out the same way in real life. There was no intruder in the night. We didn't all hug together on top of Mom and Dad's king size bed for safety. We weren't ready with our defenses for an offensive attack of some bad thing. In fact, we were quite relaxed. We had our guard let down, and our top defender, our hero, and protector was taken out of the picture without one chance to protect us. He was gone fast, and I was the second in line before I could even say "Goodbye."

I don't wish to go back and have a goodbye. I don't think it would change anything about how I feel about my relationship with my dad. That's not what hurt me the most. What hurt and keeps hurting is all the ways I tried to explain my reality to myself and holding onto those ideas even when they weren't true anymore.

"I'm afraid of being too dark for other people," I told my housemate once.

"We all know the darkness. It's not only yours," he said.

He made me feel as though I had valued my dark, my hurt, as too much, as worse than anyone else's could possibility be. It was something only I possessed. But, it's not mine exclusively. We all know the darkness around the family circle.

"There's so much more light in you than the darkness even knows." Do I know that? Do I know I have light in me? I'm saved from my darkness not because I've created some version of the world in which I take care of everyone else. No, it's because I actually have light in me too. Do I trust the light in me to be enough to overcome my darkness? I do now. I didn't before. I do now. And I can trust that because I know that I'm not the only one with the darkness. *We all know the darkness.*

The headstone for my dad's grave took months to complete. There was a place driving down the highway which passed Kohl's and Old Navy called Anderson's Monuments I had seen thousands of times along the road, but I had never *actually* seen it.

"Girls, come on, we are going to the monument shop to look at the design they have for your dad's monument."

"What are you talking about, Mom?" Allison asked. Although we knew people had stones over their gravesite, we

175

didn't understand what she meant by 'monument.'

"It's the stone, the headstone, that your dad and I will have over our graves."

"It's yours too?" Lily asked.

"We are making one for both your Dad and I." Mom answered.

"Ok, fine." I groaned, not overly interested in participating. As we pulled into the parking lot of the Anderson Monument building, we were the only car there. We walked through an elaborate sculpture garden, before winding our way to the door. A young man with a kind smile on his face immediately walked up to us.

"Hi Karen, good to see you. These must be your daughters."

"Hi John. Yes, this is Kirsten, Allison, Lily, and Heidi." She pointed to each of us in turn.

"Nice to meet you." John replied. "Follow me this way. I'll show you what we've been working on."

As we followed him, I realized what an artist he and the other people at this place were. They carved beautiful designs and figures from rock. Solid rock. There was large equipment used for hoisting the granite from one part of the space to another. In one hood, John pulled back a heavy glass door with flapping plastic to unveil a black granite stone with the word Schowalter written across the top.

Whoa.

There was something about seeing my name in stone that placed a literal weight of permanence on my shoulders in a way I denied before. Sure, it had been 8 months since Dad died, but that doesn't mean I really believed he was never coming back. I didn't believe that. The stone, though, that ripped away my disbelief in a second. That stone was permanent. That stone was going to stand, holding Dad's name, my name, for a long time.

There was what looked to me like duct tape in about 6 inch strips dispersed around the rest of the stone.

"What's that?" Allison asked.

John responded by approaching the black rock, wiping away a layer of gray dust with his hand, and peeling back one of the strips of tape. It was an eagle. He had carved an eagle soaring into the stone. He grabbed a small tool and drilled thin delicate lines into the stone adding detail and clarity to the eagle's feathers.

"What about that?" Lily asked pointing to a larger strip near the bottom of the stone.

Again, John responded by smiling and peeling back the tape to reveal the words "David Bruce."

So many times over those last few months, I'd thought, just keep going. Just one more hoop. Just get up this morning and then it'll get better. I told myself this as if I would eventually stop having to live in the world after August 11, 2007, and I would return to life before the car accident. The reality of the stone expressed "No. David Bruce isn't coming back. This new life isn't going to change. You will keep living without your dad forever."

We played this game with John until all the images carved into the stone were revealed. I felt as though everything I knew about what my life had been had been distilled and carved into the stone in front of me. The core of who I was open for passersby in the cemetery to view in mass glances amidst all the other gravestones in the area. How could there be anything left of me when all of that was gone? And yet, there I stood, breathing, thinking, and living despite the absence of what I had thought was my life.

"What do you think, girls?" Mom asked. "We had a couple different options for the color of the stone, but this one seemed the best and most affordable for us. John and I spent a lot of time figuring out the images of eagle, cow, fishing, pedigree, and the symbols to represent our lives as a family. Do you like it?"

Yes.

No.

Yes. I do like it. How could I not when it laid out the essence of who we were for all to see? Yes. It was true. It was us.

No. No. No. How could I like it? Why are we doing this? Where is Dad? Why doesn't he just come back? How can this be happening to us? No. I don't like it. How can I like it when the stone exists because of the worst thing that had ever happened to me?

"Look, we used DNA here because both of us liked genetics." She continued. "Here is a ball and bat because we met playing softball." She smiled to herself, recalling the feel of that day playing shortstop and catching the first ball of her life. "Here is where we included the miscarriage that happened before Kirsten was born, and here are each of you."

"What's that?" Heidi asked pointing to another part of the stone.

"That's a calf." John answered.

"A calf?" Heidi inquired.

"Yes, because I grew up on a dairy farm." Mom said.

"It was the best representation we could find given the small space," added John.

The longer we spent looking at the stone the more I could feel myself becoming distanced from the present. My mind was spinning with both the joy of the art John had created to represent our family and the unfathomable gouging pit of emptiness that was expanding in my gut from each second I had to face the stone.

"What else do you make here?" I asked, the words escaping my mouth without any effort or command from my brain, a self defense mechanism to change the subject to something else before I collapsed in utter pain, confusion, and inconsolable sadness.

"You can come around this way and see more of our work that's in the garden," John answered. "There are a lot of things. Mostly from orders people request, but some work are samples too to help give people an idea of all the things we could do with granite."

I moved around the stone to see the other creations in the garden. I walked along the path, circling the area once, twice, again, and again while Mom spoke with John about our headstone. Our headstone. I could no longer hold the reality of our stone inside me. Walking, I was in a fog, a dream, like the moments laying on the side of a Minnesota road or riding on gurneys through long hospital hallways; I couldn't escape or comprehend anything about the stone or granite or design or even how it could be that an accident could have such permanent effects on my life. Why? Why did our car hit another car on August 11, 2007?

"I am thinking the monument will be ready for installation at the cemetery in a few weeks. Probably early April." John explained to my mom from across the garden.

"Is that something we can watch?" she asked.

"Sure. You'd be welcome to come with me to install it. It's a fascinating physics process of pulleys and lowering the headstone onto the base in alignment."

"That sounds like a great learning experience. Girls, did you hear that? We are going to go watch John install the headstone," as excited as she was to have a teaching moment, I can only imagine the sense of regret inside her. Regretting that she had to do this. Regretting that her children would have to see this.

"I'd really love some help." John said with a smile on his face. "You girls seem like great helpers."

Great helpers. That's what we are. And that's what we need. We need to help. And we need to be helped. John knew he was walking into the most tender hurt he could find for us, and yet he asked us to help him. He knew helping would be just as powerful as being helped for us to heal.

That's the message life keeps revealing to me. Those paradoxes, helping and be helped, move and stay, light and dark, be vulnerable and be courageous, are the codes which write the movement of this world. For better or worse, I've been asked to hold them inside me, and I'm learning.

Be with people, be with myself, be with joys and be with pains all together. It's hard to be away from my mom and sisters, and yet I want space and independence. I want to move but I'm so desperate to stay, for some place and some person to hold me to stay. I don't know to what end, for what, how long, but I don't have to know.

I have the freedom, for whatever reason, so the only thing I can do is do something with it.

It has taken so much to get here, and will take so much to go from here. But for this moment, now, I feel glad. There is nothing so satisfying as the feeling I have done everything I could for the moment. Sure, it comes with missing people not in my presence, or wondering why things are how they are, those questions haven't left me, but the only person I can answer to is myself, and in the lucky moment when I have done that in this day, I am glad. I am glad. I am grateful for the call, the courage, the curiosity, the gumption, the experiment, and failure, the success, and mostly the string of moments which add up to this one. I can and will choose to risk gladness more than anything else. I will be grateful and I will be glad.

We must have the stubbornness to accept our gladness in the ruthless furnace of this world.
-Jack Gilbert

That's how I tell my story. Your turn.

The secret of change is to focus all of your energy, not on fighting the old, but on building the new.
-Dan Millman

Epilogue

One day during the summer of 1987, the Catholic singles and the medical students' softball teams were scheduled to play a game against each other. It was a sunny evening, Karen finished work, and ran home quickly to change clothes before heading to the ball field.

"Karen, you're up," Her captain said as Karen arrived at the dugout.

"What?"

"You're starting today."

"I am?"

"Yes. We are short players tonight, so you'll be shortstop."

"Oh," gasped Karen. 'I can't catch a ball to save my life. They are better off without me infield than playing short stop,' she thought.

Dave, on the other hand, was running late. He had stayed after classes to ask a question about an internal medicine case they'd seen that afternoon.

"There he is." William said as Dave, team Captain, approached the field from his car.

"Sorry, I'm late."

"No problem, Captain. We've got it all figured out anyway."

"So, where am I playing tonight?"

"We are up to bat."

"All right. I will start us off," replied Dave.

He walked to grab a bat and head over to home plate. The evening was turning out to be a bit chilly, and a cloud was temporarily covering the sun. Dave positioned himself and his bat over the base. Brushed off some of the dirt around the plate and looked toward the pitcher for his ball. 'One, two, three…' Dave counted to himself and the ball came swirling toward him.

"Ball," called the umpire. Dave straightened up and prepared for another pitch.

'One, two, three…' and the ball came sailing toward him again, faster and whizzing right over the plate.

"Strike one," said the umpire. 'All right, all right,' Dave thought. 'This next one is mine.' He readjusted his feet, gave a loose swing to the bat. 'One, two, threeeee…' *whirr SMACK!* Throwing the bat to the ground, Dave lunged toward first base. An infield pop fly ball. 'Beautiful,' he smiled to himself.

The first batter had one ball and a strike before any action happened. And when the action did happen, Karen scrambled to attention. Standing on the dirt between 2nd and 3rd base, she watched the ball go up, up, up, 'A great hit,' she noted, and then down, down, 'Oh no.' Positioning her glove above her head, she closed her eyes and heard a *thump*.

She caught it! 'I caught it!' she thought, just as the umpire called "Out!" from behind home plate.

"Great catch, Karen!" Her teammate shouted from 2nd base as she threw the ball back to her pitcher. She turned, gave him a smile, and glanced down thinking 'Maybe tonight won't be so bad after all.'

She caught it! That woman playing shortstop had caught his perfect hit! Jogging away from first and back toward the dugout, Dave knew he would have some answering to do.

"Great hit, Dave," said Vern, while Steven muttered, "If only he made it to the base," under his breath.

"You guys go get us back on the right track," Dave said settling into his spot, keeping his eye on the prize. He leaned back against the wooden wall of the dugout, paint flicking off.

"Who is that girl?" Dave asked, "Anyone know?"

"Who?" replied William.

"The woman playing shortstop."

"I know her!" said Steven. "She works in the same lab at Mayo Clinic as my girlfriend."

"What's her name?"

"Karen. Karen Weber." he replied.

"Huh," responded Dave, "Don't know her."

"Oh, she's great. I met her at a happy hour with my girlfriend a couple weeks ago."

"Huh." continued Dave.

Two weeks later, Karen left the Cytogenetics lab at the clinic for her 30 minute lunch break. A colleague had arranged for her to have lunch with a medical student who claimed he knew her from softball. Skeptical, she agreed to meet at the gardens behind the medical school at 11:30am. The garden bench was in the shape of a heart.

Karen chose a spot along the edge of the garden in the sun. "It's always so cold inside," she muttered to herself, taking in the sun's rays on her face and arms.

After ten minutes, she began to eat the lunch she packed earlier that morning. "If this guy wasn't showing up, I was at least going to enjoy an outdoor lunch," she tells us.

Another ten minutes later, still no sign of who this Dave character was. She looked up as she saw someone walking in her general direction, but he continued past her, not even asking her name. "My lunch was practically over," she says. She stood and returned the plastic ware which had previously contained her lunch back into her bag. 'I can't believe I actually agreed to this. Who is this Dave anyway?' she wondered.

"Karen?" she heard a voice from behind.

"Yes?" Turning, she saw a young man with dark brown hair and blue eyes. "I'm Dave. I'm sorry. I'm a little late, I realize," he said.

She gave him an incredulous look, asking, "A little?"

"Do you want to walk for a moment before going back to work?" he inquired hopefully.

Looking into his clear blue eyes, how could she say no?

"Sure." She answered. Dave flashed her a smile.

As my sister Heidi says, "That was when we became a possibility."

Made in the USA
San Bernardino, CA
23 January 2018